Structured Query Language

Woody R. Clermont

Published by Woody R. Clermont, 2025.

Table of Contents

Structured Query Language: SQL Concepts and Comic Relief

Woody R. Clermont

Author of *Foundations of Data Science and Statistics* and *Fusion of Law and Economics*

Book Cover by The Unrelenting Alchemist©

Published by Woody R. Clermont

Illustrations by The Unrelenting Alchemist

First edition 2025.

Preface

I have to thank Andrew J. Garnett, founder, President and CEO of Special Needs Group and Special Needs at Sea, built a global brand in the Special Needs industry. The year was 2001. He brought me on, to help usher his company into a paperless era. I was finishing law school but I had always loved computer programming, and dabbled in it every chance I had.

To understand, you have to go back in time. My father Marceau bought me several computers back in the 1980s. He first bought me a Timex Sinclair 1000, but I absolutely hated it. I eventually talked him into getting me a Commodore Vic-20 and then a Commodore 64.

I spent hours, fascinated with these computers, learning BASIC, writing programs to my heart's content. I was only 13. What did a 13 year old kid need with such things? I was not working at a software company. Yet I was hooked. After BASIC, I moved on to COBOL and PASCAL. My parents even volunteered me to tutor a college student. I was absolutely terrified. I told them, what would a 14 year old like myself, have to offer a grown man like this student? He was taking a class in FORTRAN! I did not even know FORTRAN. My parents were not taking no for an answer. I learned FORTRAN and tutored the student.

At Regis High School, I continued to study computer science as much as possible. I spent hours in the computer lab on mainframe terminals. Even in college, I loved spending time working with the IBM PC's and the Macintosh computers in the lab. After graduation and moving away from home, I was strapped for cash, and could not afford a computer. I was working as an insurance claims adjuster at Crawford and Company. My coworker taught me how to go to computer trade shows and buy the parts. He taught me to assemble my own computer from scratch.

Suffice to stay, I designed a database for my boss Andy, as well as a web interface for it. To do it, I had to learn SQL which is the subject of this book. This project did so well in 2003, we opened up the web portal to cruise lines like Norwegian, Princess, Carnival, Royal Caribbean, and Celebrity. Our business involved delivering medical equipment to passengers going on cruises (as well as airplane flights). In a post-911 world, the security and administration of the fleets were concerned with knowing what equipment were assigned to which passengers, when our employees were coming to pick up equipment, and when they were going to drop off equipment.

I was extremely happy to see my work take off and develop a life of its own. I definitely thank Andy for that experience. I did not stay in programming. I went on to become an attorney and have been practicing now for 21 years. My love for computer science however, has never died. I have an associate's degree in computer science, a bachelor of science in business information technology management, and a master of science in data analytics. Even though I do not use these degrees every day, no one could dissuade me from earning these credentials, including my SAS certifications.

I dedicate this book to my father Marceau and my son Devon. Both are very important to me. I thank my father for all that he did for me. I owe him everything. As to my son, I wish nothing but love and success to him as he embarks on his career.

I also thank Scheril who has helped me so much, to tap into my potential.

I thank God for everything. I thank the Holy Spirit and my Lord and Savior Jesus Christ.

I hope you will enjoy this book. Learning has always been lifelong and never ending for me. I trust you will come away with great knowledge after reading this work. Welcome to the journey.

Woody R. Clermont

1. World of SQL

Introduction

Structured Query Language (SQL) is the foundation of modern data management. Since its development in the 1970s by IBM researchers Donald D. Chamberlin and Raymond F. Boyce, SQL has transformed from an experimental language into the de facto standard for interacting with relational databases. Originally created to manipulate and retrieve data stored in IBM's System R, SQL was quickly adopted by industry players and standardized by ANSI and ISO. It now serves as the connective tissue in data systems across every industry.

In an increasingly data-driven world, organizations rely on SQL to bring structure and insight to their vast stores of information. The language allows developers, analysts, and data scientists to create database schemas, enforce constraints, filter records, aggregate trends, and connect complex relationships. This is all accomplished using clear, readable syntax that abstracts away the underlying complexities of database engines. SQL enables clarity in chaos—transforming unstructured, raw facts into well-defined, queryable knowledge.

What makes SQL especially powerful is its universality. Whether you're building a small web application with a backend powered by MySQL, running enterprise analytics in SQL Server or Oracle, or tinkering with lightweight apps using SQLite, you're still using SQL. Its declarative nature—focusing on "what" you want, not "how" to compute it—makes it both elegant and intuitive. From business intelligence dashboards to automated reporting systems, from e-commerce catalogs to mobile apps, SQL underpins the infrastructure of the information age.

Whether you're a beginner just opening up your first database prompt, or a seasoned professional optimizing complex joins and nested queries, learning SQL is one of the most valuable technical investments you can make. It unlocks a common language for data, empowering you to interrogate, transform, and utilize information with confidence and precision.

Main Sections

What is SQL?

SQL stands for Structured Query Language. It is a domain-specific language used to interact with relational databases, which organize data into structured tables composed of rows and columns. With SQL, you can define database schemas, enforce integrity rules, and write queries that retrieve and manipulate information with incredible flexibility. Unlike general-purpose programming languages that require detailed procedural instructions, SQL is declarative—meaning you describe the desired outcome, and the database engine determines the most efficient way to execute it.

The language includes various types of statements: Data Definition Language (DDL) for creating and modifying table structures, Data Manipulation Language (DML) for working with data inside tables, and Data Query Language (DQL) for extracting meaningful insights. SQL also includes commands for access control, transactions, and more. Whether you're fetching a customer's order history or joining datasets across time zones and continents, SQL is the bridge between raw data and human understanding.

Why SQL Still Matters

Despite the growth of NoSQL systems and alternative storage technologies like key-value stores, document databases, and graph models, SQL remains at the center of most real-world applications. It is the gold standard for structured data and is used in industries ranging from finance and healthcare to government and e-commerce. SQL excels at enforcing data integrity, supporting transactions, and enabling analytical querying, all within a consistent, standardized framework.

One of the key reasons SQL remains so dominant is its adaptability. SQL syntax and capabilities have evolved to meet the demands of modern applications: supporting JSON data types, recursive queries, full-text search, geographic information systems (GIS), and integration with programming languages and APIs. In many cases, the simplicity of SQL belies its true power—especially when optimized through indexes, views, subqueries, and complex joins. As the volume of data continues to grow, SQL scales with it through sharding, replication, and partitioning strategies implemented by modern DBMSs.

Learning SQL is not just a technical decision—it's a strategic one. Professionals with strong SQL skills are in demand across nearly every industry. The language empowers you to think critically about data and understand it at a structural level, making it an invaluable asset for analysts, engineers, data scientists, and decision-makers alike.

Overview of DBMSs

A Database Management System (DBMS) is a software application that enables users to define, create, maintain, and control access to databases. It acts as an intermediary between end-users and the physical data stored on disk, allowing for efficient management, security, and consistency. DBMSs provide tools for managing schemas, enforcing constraints, executing transactions, and controlling user permissions.

The most common types of DBMSs are relational database management systems (RDBMSs), which store data in relational tables. Among the widely used RDBMSs are:

- **MySQL:** A widely adopted open-source RDBMS, especially popular in web development. It supports standard SQL syntax and offers strong performance, scalability, and community support.
- **PostgreSQL:** An advanced open-source system with powerful features like full ACID compliance, window functions, custom types, and full-text search. Known for its standards compliance and extensibility.
- **SQL Server:** Developed by Microsoft, this DBMS uses the T-SQL dialect and integrates deeply with the Windows ecosystem and enterprise tools like Power BI and Azure.
- **Oracle:** Known for reliability, scalability, and enterprise-grade features. Oracle uses PL/SQL as its procedural extension and supports advanced features like materialized views, clustering, and fine-grained access control.
- **SQLite:** A lightweight, serverless engine embedded in applications,

ideal for mobile and desktop apps. It requires no configuration and is file-based.

Each of these systems implements the SQL standard to varying degrees while introducing unique extensions and limitations. Understanding these variations is crucial for writing portable and efficient queries. As this book progresses, we'll highlight such differences where relevant, helping you adapt your SQL knowledge across platforms.

MySQL as Our Friendly Guide (But Not Our Only Friend)

For consistency and clarity, this book primarily uses MySQL syntax and examples. MySQL's popularity, lightweight design, and intuitive behavior make it a friendly and approachable platform for learners. It offers excellent documentation, broad community support, and integration with nearly every programming language and framework. Whether you're using the command line, phpMyAdmin, or a GUI like MySQL Workbench, you'll find the ecosystem welcoming and flexible enough to support both beginners and professionals.

MySQL is also widely deployed in production environments—from small startups to large enterprises—which makes learning it not only practical but strategically useful. It powers many content management systems like WordPress, e-commerce platforms like Magento, and is frequently paired with PHP in the LAMP (Linux, Apache, MySQL, PHP) stack. Due to its simplicity, fast performance, and rich set of tools, MySQL is an excellent starting point for any aspiring data professional.

However, our journey through SQL will not be limited to a single dialect. Concepts and queries will be annotated with notes and insights about how they differ in other platforms. SQL dialects—like spoken languages—follow the same core grammar but differ in syntax, vocabulary, and idioms. For example:

- **SQL Server** (T-SQL) uses square brackets (e.g., [columnName]) and proprietary functions like GETDATE() and TOP N clauses for row limits.
- **PostgreSQL** supports robust data types like arrays and JSON, along

with advanced features like full outer joins, recursive queries, and window functions. It allows user-defined operators and supports an open extension ecosystem.

- **Oracle** uses PL/SQL and offers procedural constructs like BEGIN...END blocks and exception handling. Its architecture emphasizes performance tuning and advanced indexing methods.
- **SQLite** is minimalistic and serverless, ideal for lightweight applications like mobile apps and IoT devices. It has some limitations on concurrency and advanced joins, but its portability and zero-setup make it a go-to for embedded solutions.

We will also reference **MariaDB**, a community-driven fork of MySQL with additional features and storage engines, and **CockroachDB**, which blends traditional SQL features with distributed computing power. Cloud-native platforms such as **Amazon Redshift**, **Google BigQuery**, and **Snowflake** offer SQL-like query capabilities over massive datasets and will occasionally be discussed to show the reach of SQL across architectural paradigms.

By presenting SQL as a universal language with regional dialects, this book encourages adaptability and confidence. Whether you're crafting a local schema on SQLite or authoring distributed queries in a cloud-native warehouse, you'll recognize familiar patterns. SQL isn't just a tool for querying data—it's a shared vocabulary for understanding, modeling, and controlling structured information.

Ultimately, the goal is not to memorize the quirks of every dialect but to master the shared core of SQL and develop the flexibility to adapt your knowledge across systems. With this conceptual fluency, you'll be able to navigate any SQL-based environment with clarity and creativity.

Examples

Here are several practical examples to illustrate SQL in action across a variety of tasks, ranging from table creation to data manipulation and retrieval. These examples will give you a feel for both the structure and readability of SQL.

CREATE TABLE Example

```
CREATE TABLE employees (
    id INT PRIMARY KEY,
    name VARCHAR(100),
    department VARCHAR(50),
    hire_date DATE,
    salary DECIMAL(10,2),
    is_active BOOLEAN DEFAULT TRUE
    );
```

This statement creates an employees table with common fields such as ID, name, department, salary, hire date, and a flag for whether the employee is active. The table uses data types suitable for each field and includes a default value for is_active.

INSERT INTO Example

```
INSERT INTO employees
    (id,
    name,
    department,
    hire_date,
    salary)
    VALUES
    (1,
    'Alice Johnson',
    'Engineering',
    '2020-05-15',
    85000.00);
```

SELECT Query Example

```
SELECT name, salary
    FROM employees
    WHERE department = 'Engineering';
```

This query retrieves the names and salaries of all employees in the Engineering department. It demonstrates a basic SELECT statement with a WHERE clause.

UPDATE Example

```
UPDATE employees
    SET salary = salary * 1.05
    WHERE department = 'Engineering';
```

This statement gives a 5% raise to all Engineering employees. It uses an arithmetic operation directly within the UPDATE query.

DELETE Example

```
DELETE FROM employees
   WHERE is_active = FALSE;
```

This command removes employees who are no longer active. It's a reminder of the importance of careful filtering—DELETE operations are powerful and permanent.

ALTER TABLE Example

```
ALTER TABLE employees
   ADD email VARCHAR(255);
```

This alters the existing table to add a new column for employee emails. ALTER TABLE is useful for modifying database structure over time.

Conclusion

SQL is not just a language—it's a way of thinking about data. It's concise, powerful, and flexible. As data becomes more critical in every industry, SQL gives you the tools to harness it. Whether you're a beginner or brushing up your skills, understanding SQL means unlocking doors to insight, efficiency, and opportunity.

But more than a skill, SQL becomes a mindset—an approach to information that prioritizes clarity, structure, and precision. It forces you to think about relationships, constraints, patterns, and logic. It teaches you how to interrogate data methodically, how to draw meaningful conclusions from vast datasets, and how to construct queries that mirror your curiosity.

SQL helps you cultivate data intuition: the ability to spot redundancies, anticipate joins, structure normalized tables, and uncover hidden signals within structured formats. The more fluent you become, the more naturally you'll frame business questions as elegant queries—and the more empowered you'll be to draw meaningful conclusions in seconds, not hours.

As we move deeper into this book, you'll see how foundational SQL really is. Its syntax may be minimal, but its capacity to represent complex systems and uncover hidden trends is anything but. Whether you're cleaning raw inputs, analyzing customer behavior, or powering the backend of a global application, SQL will be your steadfast companion in the quest for data mastery.

End-of-Chapter Humor

What SQL Really Stands For:

- Slightly Questionable Language, or Sassy Query Lover? You decide.
- Some say it means Seriously Quick Linguistics. Others claim it's Simply Quite Legendary.
- Still others suggest it's Stubborn Query Language—because once you write a query, it'll keep running whether you meant to or not.
- One creative take? **Snackable Query Lollipops**. Tasty, repeatable, and if you're not careful, full of wild joins.
- Our intern once called it **Syntactically Quirky Logic**, which... might explain his last JOIN.
- Whatever the interpretation, remember: SQL may stand for Structured Query Language, but to those who use it daily, it's also a Superpower for Quantifying Life.

2. DBMS and Categories

Introduction

SQL is more than just a bag of commands—it's a structured system built on purpose and specialization. Each part of SQL exists to solve a particular problem or fulfill a particular need in working with relational databases. Without this structure, managing complex data systems would be chaotic and error-prone. The design of SQL reflects the way we think about data as a resource—something to define, manipulate, secure, and query with precision.

At the heart of SQL's structure is the relational model, which organizes data into tables made up of rows and columns. Each column is known as a **field**, representing a particular attribute (like name, date, or status), and each row is a **record**, containing the specific values for one entry. To uniquely identify records, most tables include a **primary key**, often implemented as a sequential **Record ID**. This key ensures that even if all other field values are duplicated, each record remains uniquely distinguishable. These keys are critical when establishing **relationships** between tables, which is where the concept of **cardinality** comes in—defining how rows in one table relate to rows in another (e.g., one-to-many, many-to-many).

The beauty of SQL lies in how it organizes tasks into five sublanguages: Data Definition Language (DDL), Data Manipulation Language (DML), Data Control Language (DCL), Transaction Control Language (TCL), and Data Query Language (DQL). These categories aren't just theoretical—they determine which SQL tools you use depending on what you're trying to accomplish. Are you setting up a database schema from scratch? You'll use DDL. Are you updating thousands of records with new information? DML is your friend. Each sublanguage focuses on a different aspect of data interaction.

These categories help developers, analysts, and database administrators understand how to structure queries and what tools to reach for when tackling specific problems. They also improve clarity in communication and maintainability in code. In large teams or long-term projects, knowing whether a statement is part of DML or TCL isn't just trivia—it determines how your work integrates into systems of security, backups, logging, and automation.

Mastering this layered organization of SQL—grounded in concepts like records, fields, keys, and cardinality—is key to mastering the language itself.

Understanding DBMS, Tables, Fields, and Records

A Database Management System (DBMS) is sophisticated software that enables users to define, create, maintain, and control access to databases. It handles tasks such as storing data, ensuring consistency, enforcing data integrity, and providing secure access. Without a DBMS, managing vast amounts of structured data would be nearly impossible. DBMSs automate many complex processes like indexing, transaction management, and backup routines, offering a user-friendly interface and a powerful backend for data management.

Modern DBMSs fall into several categories, with relational DBMSs (RDBMSs) being the most commonly used. These include MySQL, PostgreSQL, Microsoft SQL Server, Oracle Database, and SQLite. They adhere to the relational model where data is organized into tables and relationships are defined among them. These systems allow data to be queried using SQL and often include advanced features like stored procedures, triggers, constraints, and replication.

At its core, a relational database is composed of **tables**. These tables resemble spreadsheets, made up of horizontal **rows** and vertical **columns**—but the resemblance stops at the surface. Unlike spreadsheets, tables enforce data types, relationships, and integrity rules. Tables are designed to represent entities such as customers, products, orders, or employees.

- Each **column** in a table is called a **field**. It stores a specific type of data for all records in that column. Fields define what kind of information the table holds, such as a person's name, a price, or a timestamp.
- Each **row** is a **record**. A record represents a unique instance or entry in the table. For example, a row in a customer table might represent an individual customer with all their related data.

Think of a table as a structured form: the fields are the blanks to be filled out, and each record is one completed form. This structure allows data to be easily searched, sorted, filtered, updated, or joined with other tables.

Example: Customer Table

Name	Phone	Email
Amy	555-1234	amy@example.com
Bob	555-5678	bob@example.com
David	555-8765	david@example.com
Kevin	555-3456	kevin@example.com

In this table:

- The columns Name, Phone, and Email represent **fields.**
- Each row—such as Amy's or Bob's—is a **record** that captures the complete data for one customer.

A field contains one type of information, but a record contains all types relevant to one entity. Together, fields and records allow a table to encapsulate the richness and variety of structured data. When you query a database, you're typically asking for specific records that match criteria based on field values.

Field Attributes and Properties

Fields aren't just containers—they can have attributes like data type (e.g., TEXT, INT, DATE), constraints (e.g., NOT NULL, UNIQUE), and default values. These properties enforce data integrity and ensure that every record in the table is meaningful and valid. Advanced systems even allow computed fields or validation rules.

For instance:

- The Phone field might have a constraint to match a specific format.
- The Email field might be marked UNIQUE to prevent duplicates.

These attributes prevent bad data from entering the system, reducing downstream errors and increasing trust in the data.

Record ID

Each record is uniquely identified by a special value called the **Record ID** or **Primary Key**. This field guarantees that every record is distinct, even if all other fields contain identical values. The Record ID is often an auto-incrementing integer that starts at 1 and increases sequentially with each new row added.

- Record IDs ensure fast lookups and allow the system to link tables through foreign keys.
- Even if a record is deleted, its ID is never reused in that table. This preserves referential integrity across the system.

Consider a case where multiple customers have the same name and email. The Record ID is what distinguishes them in the system. This ID can also be used to track relationships between tables (e.g., which orders belong to which customer), to handle edits and deletions securely, and to maintain historical logs.

Record IDs are foundational to relational databases. They are essential to ensuring consistency, enabling joins, preventing redundancy, and maintaining order in otherwise complex datasets.

Cardinality and Relationships

In relational databases, data is spread across multiple tables to reduce redundancy and maintain integrity. But real-world systems are interconnected, customers place orders, employees belong to departments, and students enroll in courses. To represent these relationships, database designers use keys and establish links between tables. This is where the concept of **cardinality** becomes essential.

Cardinality defines how many instances of one entity relate to instances of another. In simple terms, it answers the question: “How many of these relate to how many of those?” Understanding cardinality enables database designers to correctly model associations and optimize data retrieval. Poorly defined cardinality can lead to data anomalies, inefficient queries, and logical inconsistencies.

Mapping Cardinality

Mapping cardinality, or cardinality ratio, refers to the number of relationships between tuples (rows) in two tables. It plays a crucial role in describing binary relationships but can also apply to complex, multi-table relationships. There are four fundamental types:

- **One-to-One (1:1):** Each row in Table A is associated with one and only one row in Table B, and vice versa. This is often used to separate sensitive data (like login credentials) from a main table. Example: A person has one passport, and each passport is assigned to one person.
- **One-to-Many (1:N):** A single row in Table A can be associated with multiple rows in Table B, but each row in Table B maps to only one in Table A. Example: One professor teaches many classes, but each class has one professor.
- **Many-to-One (N:1):** The reverse of one-to-many. Many records in Table A refer to a single record in Table B. Example: Multiple employees report to one manager.
- **Many-to-Many (M:N):** Each row in Table A can relate to multiple rows in Table B, and each row in Table B can relate to multiple rows in Table A. These require an intermediary junction table. Example: Students enroll in multiple courses; each course includes multiple students.

Examples of Mapping Cardinality

- **1:1** — Each country has one capital city; each capital city belongs to one country.
- **1:N** — A library has many books, but each book belongs to one library.
- **N:1** — Multiple appointments are scheduled with one doctor.
- **M:N** — Many products are part of many customer orders.

Visualizing Relationships with ER Diagrams

Entity-Relationship (ER) diagrams visually model cardinality. For instance:

- A **crow's foot** at one end of a relationship line denotes "many."
- A **single line** or bar indicates "one."

These visuals make it easier to understand constraints and participation. Total participation is shown by a bold line; partial participation by a regular line. Accurate visual modeling of cardinality helps avoid misunderstandings in collaborative environments.

Impact of Cardinality on Schema Design

Understanding cardinality guides key decisions in database structure:

- Whether to include a foreign key in one table or use a junction table
- Whether normalization should be enforced or partially relaxed
- How indexes should be created to optimize lookups and joins
- Whether constraints like UNIQUE or NOT NULL are appropriate

For example, in a one-to-one relationship with total participation on both sides, you can merge both tables. But in a many-to-many setup, you must create an intersection table with foreign keys referencing each primary table.

Cardinality in Query Performance and Indexing

Beyond data modeling, cardinality affects query performance.

- **High cardinality** columns (e.g., Social Security Number) contain mostly unique values. These are ideal candidates for indexing.
- **Low cardinality** columns (e.g., gender, Boolean flags) may not benefit as much from indexing but are still important in filtering and grouping.

Query optimizers use cardinality estimates to determine the most efficient execution plans. Misjudging cardinality can result in full-table scans, poor join algorithms, or suboptimal sort operations.

Why Cardinality Matters

Understanding cardinality helps:

- Determine foreign key placement
- Design efficient and normalized schemas
- Avoid update, insert, and delete anomalies
- Ensure data reflects real-world business rules
- Optimize database storage and access speed

Cardinality is the heartbeat of relational modeling. Without it, your database structure may work, but it won't be elegant—or efficient.

DDL, DML, DCL, TCL, DQL

The Five Sublanguages

- **Data Definition Language (DDL)** — DDL is responsible for defining and managing the structure of database objects like tables, views, schemas, and indexes. It lays the foundation for how data will be stored and organized. Common DDL commands include CREATE, ALTER, DROP, and TRUNCATE. These operations are structural and usually require elevated permissions because they affect the schema itself. Once defined with DDL, tables become the vessels through which data is stored and accessed.
- **Data Manipulation Language (DML)** — DML is used to modify the actual data stored in the database. This includes adding new records, updating existing ones, and deleting obsolete data. The primary commands in this category are INSERT, UPDATE, and DELETE. DML is what allows your application to interact with live data and perform day-to-day transactions. These commands typically

occur after the structure is already defined by DDL.

- **Data Control Language (DCL)** — DCL is concerned with setting and managing user permissions and access control within the database. It determines who can view or change certain parts of the database. Key DCL commands include GRANT and REVOKE. These are essential for maintaining security and protecting sensitive data from unauthorized access. DCL is crucial in multi-user environments where roles and privileges must be clearly defined.
- **Transaction Control Language (TCL)** — TCL ensures that groups of DML statements are executed safely and reliably as transactions. This helps maintain data integrity, especially in multi-step operations. Commands such as COMMIT, ROLLBACK, and SAVEPOINT allow you to confirm, undo, or segment changes as needed. TCL is vital in applications where accuracy is non-negotiable, such as banking or order processing systems. It makes your database operations both atomic and predictable.
- **Data Query Language (DQL)** — DQL is focused on retrieving data from the database using structured queries. The main command here is SELECT, which allows users to filter, sort, aggregate, and analyze data. DQL gives you powerful ways to transform raw rows into meaningful information. While it doesn't modify the data, it's arguably the most frequently used category in day-to-day analysis. Through DQL, SQL becomes a window into the story your data is trying to tell.

When and Why to Use Each

Each category plays a specific role in interacting with relational databases:

- Use **DDL** when you're designing or modifying the structure of your database. Think of it as the blueprinting phase.
- Use **DML** when you're actively working with the data—adding customers, updating records, or deleting old logs.
- Use **DCL** when you're setting permissions, controlling who can read,

write, or delete data.

- Use **TCL** when you're managing multiple DML actions as a single atomic transaction.
- Use **DQL** when you're querying data—filtering, sorting, aggregating, and analyzing it.

Understanding when to use each sublanguage builds the foundation for writing efficient, organized, and secure SQL code.

Syntax Examples for Each

DDL Example:

```
CREATE TABLE users (
id INT PRIMARY KEY,
username VARCHAR(50),
signup_date DATE
);
```

DML Example:

```
INSERT INTO users (id, username, signup_date)
VALUES (1, 'admin', '2025-01-01');
```

DCL Example:

```
GRANT SELECT, INSERT ON users
TO reporting_user;
```

TCL Example:

```
BEGIN;
UPDATE users SET username = 'admin2'
WHERE id = 1;
ROLLBACK;
```

DQL Example:

```
SELECT username
FROM users
WHERE signup_date > '2025-01-01';
```

Examples

These mini examples show how the five SQL categories work together to build and manage a fully functioning database. Think of each category as a toolkit:

- DDL gives you the hammer and nails to build.
- DML lets you fill your structure with meaningful content.

- DCL controls the locks on the doors.
- TCL manages what happens when someone wants to renovate.
- DQL gives you the flashlight to find exactly what you're looking for.

Conclusion

Understanding these categories is the key to mastering SQL. Each command you write fits into one of these functional domains. Once you understand what category you're working in, your queries become more purposeful, your errors easier to debug, and your thinking more aligned with how relational databases are designed.

End-of-Chapter Humor

Dinner Party Analogy:

- **DDL** sets the table and picks the furniture.
- **DML** brings the food and serves the guests.
- **DCL** decides who gets an invite and who's stuck outside.
- **TCL** intervenes when someone spills the wine and offers to reset the whole evening.
- **DQL** just wants to know who brought the apple pie.

3. MySQL

Introduction

MySQL is one of the most widely used open-source relational database management systems (RDBMS) across the globe. Trusted by developers, administrators, and data professionals alike, it powers everything from small blogs to massive e-commerce platforms. Whether you're building a new web application or supporting legacy infrastructure, chances are you'll encounter MySQL at some point in your career.

What sets MySQL apart is its unique combination of performance, flexibility, and community support. It delivers high-speed query[1] processing, strong data integrity,[2] and compatibility with virtually every major programming language and operating system. It's also incredibly accessible—completely free to use under the GNU General Public License and supported by a vibrant open-source community that regularly contributes updates, fixes, and improvements.

In this chapter, we'll explore the fundamentals of getting started with MySQL. This includes how to install the MySQL server on different operating systems, how to configure a secure and usable environment, and how to connect via various tools and interfaces like PHP[3] for example. You'll learn how to use the command-line client, graphical tools like MySQL Workbench, and browser-based interfaces such as phpMyAdmin.[4]

But this chapter isn't just about setup. We'll also walk through essential concepts such as selecting a database, creating tables, inserting records, and managing users and permissions. Whether you're a beginner looking to understand your first database system or a seasoned developer refreshing your knowledge, this chapter will give you the practical grounding you need.

By the end, you won't just have MySQL running—you'll know your way around it. You'll understand the difference between administrative tasks and query operations, how to troubleshoot common issues, and which workflows will help you get the most out of MySQL. Think of this chapter as your launchpad into the world of SQL-powered development.

Installing MySQL

Platform Options

MySQL is designed to be highly portable and works seamlessly across major operating systems, including Windows, macOS, and various Linux distributions. This cross-platform compatibility makes it an ideal choice for developers working in heterogeneous environments or transitioning between systems.

Windows: On Windows, MySQL can be installed using the MySQL Installer, a graphical wizard provided by Oracle. This tool allows users to install not only the MySQL Server but also optional components such as MySQL Workbench, MySQL Shell, documentation, and connectors for languages like Python, Java, and C++. The installer handles dependency checks, user setup, configuration, and service initialization. Alternatively, advanced users may download the ZIP Archive version for manual setup and configuration via the command line.

macOS: On macOS, MySQL can be installed via two common methods: the native MySQL DMG package available from the official website, or the more developer-oriented route using Homebrew, the popular package manager. With Homebrew, installation is as simple as:

```
brew install mysql
```

After installation, the service can be started with:

```
brew services start mysql
```

macOS users also benefit from a robust GUI ecosystem, including MySQL Workbench, Sequel Pro (for legacy users), and TablePlus.

Linux: Linux users have multiple options depending on their distribution. On Debian-based systems like Ubuntu, MySQL can be installed using the `apt` package manager:

```
sudo apt update
sudo apt install mysql-server
```

For Red Hat-based distributions like CentOS and Fedora, the `dnf` or `yum` package managers are used:

```
sudo yum install mysql-server
```

After installation, the MySQL service can be enabled and started using systemd:

```
sudo systemctl enable mysqld
```

```
sudo systemctl start mysqld
```

Docker: Another increasingly popular method of deploying MySQL is via Docker. This is particularly useful for development and testing environments, CI/CD pipelines, or situations where isolated containerized instances are preferred. A basic MySQL container can be spun up with:

```
docker run—name mysql-container
-e MYSQL_ROOT_PASSWORD=my-secret
-d mysql:latest
```

Docker volumes can be mounted to preserve data, and different configurations can be passed through environment variables or configuration files.

Cloud Platforms: In addition to local installations, MySQL is available as a managed service on most major cloud platforms. Amazon RDS for MySQL, Google Cloud SQL, and Azure Database for MySQL offer scalable, maintenance-free deployments with automatic backups, monitoring, and high availability options. These platforms allow users to focus on schema design and query optimization while abstracting server maintenance and configuration.

Choosing the Right Option: The best platform for MySQL depends on your use case:

- For desktop-based development, Windows and macOS provide rich GUI tools and fast local runtimes.
- For production servers and automated scripts, Linux offers unmatched performance, stability, and package management.
- For scalable web applications and high-availability systems, cloud-hosted MySQL services reduce operational complexity.
- For testing and portability, Docker provides fast provisioning and teardown of clean MySQL environments.

No matter your choice, MySQL's flexibility ensures a consistent experience. Most SQL syntax, command-line tools, and libraries remain compatible across environments, allowing you to switch between platforms with minimal friction. The official MySQL documentation provides platform-specific guides, and an active community ensures that virtually every installation problem has a solution just a search away.

Installation Steps (Example: macOS with Homebrew)

Installing MySQL on macOS using Homebrew is one of the easiest and most reproducible methods, especially for developers working in terminal-heavy environments. Here's a step-by-step breakdown of the process, along with explanations and best practices:

Step 1: Update Homebrew

Before installing any packages, it's always a good idea to ensure that Homebrew is up to date. This prevents dependency issues and ensures you're installing the latest versions.

```
brew update
```

This command fetches the latest package definitions and formulae from the Homebrew repositories.

Step 2: Install MySQL

Now that Homebrew is up to date, install MySQL with the following command:

```
brew install mysql
```

Homebrew will download the MySQL binaries, perform necessary compilation if required, and install the service into your local system path. Depending on your machine and network speed, this step may take a few minutes.

Step 3: Start MySQL as a Background Service

Once MySQL is installed, you can start it as a background service that launches on system startup:

```
brew services start mysql
```

This will run MySQL in the background and ensure that it remains active across reboots. If you prefer to start MySQL manually when needed, you can run:

```
mysql.server start
```

Step 4: Run the Secure Installation Script

The initial installation comes with some default settings that should be hardened for better security, especially if the database is being used in production or shared environments.

```
mysql_secure_installation
```

This interactive script walks you through essential configuration options:

- Setting a root password
- Removing anonymous users
- Disallowing root login remotely
- Removing the test database
- Reloading the privilege tables

Answering "Yes" to most of these prompts is typically the safest option.

Step 5: Verify the Installation

To ensure everything is installed and running correctly, try logging into MySQL:

```
mysql -u root -p
```

You'll be prompted for the root password you set during the secure installation script. If successful, you'll enter the MySQL command-line client and see a prompt that looks like this:

```
mysql>
```

From here, you can run SQL commands such as:

```
SHOW DATABASES;
```

Optional: Stop or Restart the MySQL Service

If you ever need to stop the MySQL service:

```
brew services stop mysql
```

To restart it (e.g., after a configuration change):

```
brew services restart mysql
```

Summary

Installing MySQL via Homebrew simplifies setup and ongoing management. It aligns with macOS development workflows and ensures quick version upgrades and service controls. Whether you're running a personal project or prototyping a full-stack web app, this installation method gets you up and running with minimal friction.

Connecting to MySQL

Command Line

The command-line interface (CLI) offers a fast and powerful way to interact with your MySQL server. It's a favorite among developers and administrators for tasks like automation, scripting, and remote access.

To launch the MySQL monitor, open your terminal and run:

```
mysql -u root -p
```

The `-u root` flag specifies that you're logging in as the root user, and the `-p` flag tells MySQL to prompt you for a password. After entering the correct password, you'll see a familiar prompt:

```
mysql>
```

From here, you can run SQL queries directly. For example:

```
SHOW DATABASES;
```

will list all databases visible to the root user. This interface also supports tab-completion, command history, and scripting via .sql files.

Graphical Interfaces

While the command line is versatile, many users prefer graphical tools for visualization and ease of navigation. These interfaces are especially helpful for beginners or when working with complex schemas.

- **MySQL Workbench:** This is the official GUI provided by Oracle. It offers an integrated environment for SQL development, database modeling, server configuration, and user management. You can view entity-relationship diagrams, write and execute SQL scripts, and even schedule backups.

- **phpMyAdmin:** A lightweight, web-based alternative that allows you to manage MySQL databases from any browser. Popular with LAMP stack developers, it's often pre-installed on shared hosting environments. Tasks like importing/exporting databases, adding tables, or tweaking columns are made simple with its intuitive interface.
- **DBeaver / HeidiSQL:** These third-party clients are versatile and support multiple DBMSs (e.g., PostgreSQL, Oracle, SQL Server). They provide query editors, ER diagram viewers, user permission panels, and more. Ideal for power users juggling various databases across projects.

Each interface connects to your database via host address, port (typically 3306), and authentication credentials. They all allow query writing, table browsing, data manipulation, and user access control.

Basic MySQL Workflow

A common MySQL development session follows a logical progression: create a database, select it, define tables, then populate and query them. Here's how to get started:

Create a Database

This statement creates a new database named bookstore:

```
CREATE DATABASE bookstore;
```

This is typically the first step in a new project. It defines a container in which all your tables and views will live. You can specify character sets and collations too:

```
CREATE DATABASE bookstore
CHARACTER SET utf8mb4 COLLATE utf8mb4_unicode_ci;
```

Use a Database

Once the database is created, select it so subsequent operations apply to it:

```
USE bookstore;
```

This sets the context for all table creation, data insertion, and queries to follow. You can only work within one database at a time in a given session.

Create a Table

Now that you're inside the bookstore database, you can define a books table:

```
CREATE TABLE books (
id INT AUTO_INCREMENT PRIMARY KEY,
title VARCHAR(255) NOT NULL,
author VARCHAR(100) NOT NULL,
published_year INT,
genre VARCHAR(50),
in_stock BOOLEAN DEFAULT TRUE
);
```

This schema includes fields for the book title, author, year of publication, genre, and availability status. The id field acts as a **primary key**, uniquely identifying each record. AUTO_INCREMENT ensures that each new record receives a unique numeric identifier automatically.

You can modify or extend this table later using ALTER TABLE commands, and you can view its structure using:

```
DESCRIBE books;
```

Insert Data

```
INSERT INTO books (title, author, published_year)
VALUES ('1984', 'George Orwell', 1949);
```

Query Data

```
SELECT * FROM books;
```

MySQL User Management

```
CREATE USER 'librarian'@'localhost'
IDENTIFIED BY 'securepassword';
GRANT SELECT, INSERT, UPDATE
ON bookstore.* TO 'librarian'@'localhost';
```

This creates a new user with limited permissions on the "bookstore" database.

Best Practices for Beginners

- Use SHOW DATABASES; and SHOW TABLES; to explore your schema.
- Always use LIMIT when experimenting with SELECT to avoid returning massive datasets.
- Practice using EXPLAIN to understand query performance.
- Use DESCRIBE tablename; to view the structure of a table.

MySQL Data Types (Version 8.0)

String Data Types

Data Type	Description
CHAR(size)	Fixed-length string (0 to 255 characters). Default is 1.
VARCHAR(size)	Variable-length string (0 to 65535 characters).
BINARY(size)	Like CHAR(), but stores binary byte strings.
VARBINARY(size)	Like VARCHAR(), but stores binary byte strings.
TINYBLOB	Binary Large Object, max 255 bytes.
TINYTEXT	Holds up to 255 characters.
TEXT	Holds up to 65,535 bytes.
BLOB	Binary data, up to 65,535 bytes.
MEDIUMTEXT	Holds up to 16,777,215 characters.
MEDIUMBLOB	Binary data, up to 16,777,215 bytes.
LONGTEXT	Holds up to 4,294,967,295 characters.
LONGBLOB	Binary data, up to 4,294,967,295 bytes.
ENUM(val1,...)	One value from a defined list (up to 65535 values).
SET(val1,...)	Zero or more values from a list (up to 64 values).

Numeric Data Types

Data Type	Description
BIT(size)	Bit-value storage. 1 to 64 bits.
TINYINT(size)	Small integer: -128 to 127 (signed), 0 to 255 (unsigned).
BOOL / BOOLEAN	Treated as TINYINT(1). Zero is false, nonzero is true.
SMALLINT(size)	-32,768 to 32,767 (signed), 0 to 65,535 (unsigned).
MEDIUMINT(size)	-8,388,608 to 8,388,607 (signed).
INT / INTEGER(size)	-2,147,483,648 to 2,147,483,647 (signed).
BIGINT(size)	-9.2 quintillion to 9.2 quintillion (signed).
FLOAT(p)	Approx. 7-digit precision if p=24. FLOAT or DOUBLE based on p.
DOUBLE / DOUBLE PRECISION(size,d)	Floating-point with specified precision.
DECIMAL(size,d) / DEC(size,d)	Exact fixed-point values. Up to 65 digits, 30 decimals.

Date and Time Data Types

Data Type	Description
DATE	Format: YYYY-MM-DD. Range: 1000-01-01 to 9999-12-31.
DATETIME(fsp)	Full timestamp: YYYY-MM-DD hh:mm:ss. Supports fractional seconds.
TIMESTAMP(fsp)	Like DATETIME, but tied to Unix epoch. Used for versioning and default times.
TIME(fsp)	Time of day. Range: -838:59:59 to 838:59:59.
YEAR	Four-digit year: 1901 to 2155, and 0000.

Conclusion

MySQL offers a clean and efficient entry point into SQL-based development. Whether you're prototyping a web app or supporting analytics dashboards, its accessibility and power make it an excellent first RDBMS. The skills you build here will serve you well across any SQL platform. Personally, I first began to learn SQL in a Perl[5] environment, trying to access a Microsoft Access database. I did not have educational training in the subject area, and was self-taught. Eventually I needed to expand beyond Access, and the other RDMBS options were too expensive. Then I stumbled onto the free MySQL, and it changed everything for me.

Beyond its beginner-friendly features, MySQL is a battle-tested engine used by companies of all sizes—from startups deploying WordPress blogs to global enterprises managing millions of transactions per day. Its versatility, strong documentation, and open-source nature make it an ideal sandbox for learning as well as a robust platform for production.

Learning MySQL means more than just memorizing syntax. You're cultivating the ability to think relationally: to design data models, structure queries for performance, and build repeatable workflows that scale. From defining tables and writing joins to managing users and securing data, each interaction deepens your fluency in a language that powers the modern data-driven world.

As you continue your journey through SQL, keep MySQL close. It will not only help you experiment and test ideas quickly, but also give you the practical grounding you need to transition into more specialized tools like PostgreSQL, SQL Server, or cloud-native engines like Amazon RDS and Google Cloud SQL. MySQL isn't just a stepping stone—it's a dependable partner in real-world data management.

End-of-Chapter Humor

Why did the MySQL table get kicked out of the party?

- Because it couldn't commit!
- And every time it rolled back, it forgot what happened.

I mentioned Perl earlier in the chapter, and provided its retronym. Its creator Larry Wall also jokingly suggested it could stand for "Pathologically Eclectic Rubbish Lister". Stay tuned—next chapter we join forces with CREATE, SELECT, and friends as we build your very first project!

4. DDL

Introduction

Data Definition Language (DDL) is a critical part of SQL that allows users to define and modify the structure of database objects. These objects include tables, schemas, views, indexes, and constraints. Without DDL, there would be no framework within which data could be organized or manipulated. In this chapter, we explore the commands that shape the skeleton of any relational database. Think of DDL as the architectural phase in database design, laying the foundation before any data can live inside.

DDL is where all meaningful database work begins. Just like blueprints precede the construction of a building, DDL commands like CREATE, ALTER, and DROP prepare the environment where information will be housed. These commands determine what kind of data can be stored, how it will be structured, and what rules must be followed for its organization. For example, defining a table isn't simply about declaring column names—it's also about specifying data types, constraints like NOT NULL or UNIQUE, and relationships to other tables via primary and foreign keys.

DDL also plays an essential role in planning for scalability and integrity. When a database is properly designed using DDL principles, it minimizes redundancy, ensures consistency, and supports complex relationships between entities. For developers and data architects alike, DDL provides the necessary precision to express real-world concepts in digital form. Whether you're building a simple contacts database or a multi-layered enterprise system, the robustness of your DDL design will shape your application's future stability and performance.

Moreover, understanding DDL isn't just about issuing one-off commands—it's about adopting a mindset that considers structure as a first-class priority. It empowers you to think critically about data flow, enforce business logic at the schema level, and collaborate more effectively in teams where database schemas may be shared across applications. Mastery of DDL is a prerequisite for building secure, efficient, and well-governed data ecosystems.

In this chapter, we'll look at each DDL command in detail and walk through practical use cases that mirror what developers face in real-world projects.

Historical Background of DDL

The concept of Data Definition Language has its roots in the early development of relational database theory, primarily credited to Edgar F. Codd's landmark work in the 1970s. As relational models gained traction, there emerged a need for a standardized way to define the structure of tables, enforce relationships, and manage the metadata that underpins any database system. SQL, developed by IBM in the System R project, formally introduced the idea of separating data definition from data manipulation—a design that persists in virtually all modern RDBMS platforms.

In the early days, schema definitions were tightly coupled with application logic, leading to brittle systems that were difficult to maintain or scale. The introduction of DDL allowed for declarative, centralized schema design. This paradigm shift made it possible to define databases abstractly, with clear boundaries between structure and behavior. As SQL matured, so did the syntax and capability of DDL, expanding from basic table creation to include powerful features like cascading constraints, partitioning, virtual columns, and schema evolution tools.

Over time, DDL became more than just a set of commands—it evolved into a language of design. The commands you write in DDL don't just define structure; they communicate intent to other developers, signal constraints to application frameworks, and even drive automation in DevOps workflows. Today, understanding DDL is essential for everything from designing scalable APIs to generating entity-relationship diagrams and reverse engineering legacy databases.

Modern DDL continues to expand its reach. In systems like MySQL, PostgreSQL, and Oracle, new DDL features now integrate with user roles, transactions, and temporal tables. Some platforms even allow version-controlled DDL scripts for continuous integration and automated schema migration. The separation of DDL from other SQL sublanguages remains a cornerstone of clean, modular database development—a testament to the enduring utility of this foundational concept.

Key DDL Commands

CREATE

The CREATE command is used to define and instantiate new database objects within the system. While the most common application of CREATE is for table definitions, it can also be employed to construct schemas, views, stored procedures, indexes, triggers, and even entire databases. The command sets the initial structure and metadata for a given object, defining its fields, data types, constraints, and default values. Creating objects is a fundamental step in modeling a relational database system—it determines how data will be stored, accessed, and enforced through rules. A well-designed CREATE statement ensures logical consistency, future scalability, and alignment with application requirements.

Example: Create a Table

```
CREATE TABLE employees (
id INT PRIMARY KEY AUTO_INCREMENT,
name VARCHAR(100) NOT NULL,
department VARCHAR(50),
salary DECIMAL(10,2) CHECK (salary > 0),
hire_date DATE DEFAULT CURRENT_DATE
);
```

This defines a new table named employees with a primary key that auto-increments, appropriate data types, a CHECK constraint on salary, and a default value for hire_date. Such structure reflects best practices in relational schema design, minimizing invalid data and promoting readability.

ALTER

The ALTER command is essential for modifying existing database objects without destroying or recreating them. It allows the addition or deletion of columns, the modification of column data types, renaming tables or columns, and the addition or removal of constraints. This command is frequently used during development and schema evolution, making it invaluable in dynamic environments where requirements change over time. ALTER can help preserve data while modernizing schema definitions or accommodating application updates. It is often paired with version control systems to track changes across deployment environments.

Example: Add a Column

```
ALTER TABLE employees
ADD email VARCHAR(255) UNIQUE;
```

This adds a new column named email and ensures that its values are unique across records.

Example: Modify a Column

```
ALTER TABLE employees
MODIFY salary DECIMAL(12,2);
```

This modifies the salary column to support larger salary figures and greater numeric precision.

DROP

The DROP command is used to delete database objects entirely, removing both their structure and contents. Objects that can be dropped include tables, views, procedures, functions, indexes, and even entire databases. Because DROP is irreversible (outside of a transaction-safe DBMS with backup mechanisms), it should be used with extreme caution. Dropping objects is typically reserved for cleanup operations, migration tasks, or deprecating outdated modules. Always ensure that backups and dependency checks are in place before executing this command.

Example: Drop a Table

```
DROP TABLE IF EXISTS employees;
```

Using IF EXISTS prevents an error if the table does not exist, offering a layer of protection in deployment scripts.

TRUNCATE

The TRUNCATE command removes all rows from a table while preserving the table's schema, indexes, and constraints. Unlike DELETE, it does not generate individual row delete logs and cannot generally be rolled back unless within a transactional context on supported systems. TRUNCATE is extremely fast and often used for resetting test data, clearing temporary caches, or preparing tables for bulk inserts. It reinitializes the auto-increment counter (if applicable) and is optimized for performance in large datasets. Still, use caution—TRUNCATE is not the same as DELETE and behaves differently with respect to triggers and logging.

Example: Truncate a Table

```
TRUNCATE TABLE employees;
```

All rows in the employees table will be removed, but the table structure and schema definition remain intact.

Constraints in DDL

Constraints are used in DDL to enforce rules on the data in tables. These rules are applied at the column or table level and ensure integrity, consistency, and validity of data. SQL provides a suite of constraints to govern how data is inserted, updated, or deleted. Applying constraints prevents common issues like duplicate keys, invalid dates, or orphaned foreign keys. Designing tables with appropriate constraints is a hallmark of robust database design.

- **PRIMARY KEY** - Uniquely identifies each record and prevents duplicates. Often paired with AUTO_INCREMENT in MySQL.
- **FOREIGN KEY** - Creates a link to a column in another table, enforcing relational integrity.
- **UNIQUE** - Ensures that all values in a column are different; often used for emails or usernames.
- **NOT NULL** - Prevents a column from storing NULL values.
- **CHECK** - Limits the value range allowed in a column, such as CHECK (age >= 18).

Example: Constraint within CREATE

```
CREATE TABLE departments (
dept_id INT PRIMARY KEY,
dept_name VARCHAR(100) NOT NULL UNIQUE,
floor INT CHECK (floor BETWEEN 1 AND 10)
);
```

This statement ensures that each department has a unique name, non-null value, and resides on a valid floor level.

Schema Management

A schema is a logical container that holds tables, views, indexes, procedures, and more, allowing better organization and permission management. In MySQL, a schema is synonymous with a database. Schema management with DDL involves creating, modifying, or removing these containers to isolate or structure applications. Logical separation using schemas can help in multi-tenant applications or for segmenting environments like dev, test, and prod. Proper schema planning simplifies migrations, backups, access control, and system maintenance.

Example: Create a Schema

```
CREATE SCHEMA IF NOT EXISTS company;
```

This command creates a new schema named company only if it doesn't already exist.

Example: Use a Schema

```
USE company;
```

Switches the current context to the company schema so that all subsequent operations apply to it.

Best Practices

- **Backups Are Non-Negotiable:** Always back up your data and schema before executing DDL operations, especially destructive ones like DROP, TRUNCATE, or drastic ALTERs. Losing structural metadata or reference integrity due to a mistyped command can be catastrophic. Use full and incremental backups in conjunction with logical dumps (like mysqldump) to maintain flexibility. In production environments, integrate automatic backups before migrations. Backups should also be tested periodically for restorability.
- **Use Conditional Clauses:** Include IF EXISTS and IF NOT EXISTS clauses in CREATE, DROP, and ALTER commands to safeguard scripts from crashing during re-runs or CI/CD pipelines. This ensures idempotency and allows repeated deployment scripts without side effects. It also improves developer confidence and minimizes human intervention. For example, CREATE TABLE IF NOT EXISTS avoids

exceptions when run against an already-initialized schema. Similarly, DROP TABLE IF EXISTS adds protection against "object not found" errors.

- **Avoid DDL and DML Mixing:** DDL operations often cause implicit commits in many RDBMSs, making them incompatible with transactional DML flows. Mixing the two in a single transaction can lead to partial changes that are hard to roll back or recover from. If you must perform both, separate them into discrete operations with commit boundaries. Check DBMS-specific documentation (e.g., MySQL, PostgreSQL, SQL Server) for transactional DDL support. For example, MySQL treats most DDL statements as non-transactional.
- **Version Control and Change Tracking:** Maintain detailed logs and comments on all DDL changes using schema migration tools like Flyway, Liquibase, or Alembic. These tools allow developers to manage evolving database schemas systematically and support rollback/versioning. In team environments, version control eliminates "schema drift" across development, staging, and production. Commenting inline with each DDL change also aids long-term maintainability. Consider pairing migrations with changelogs in Git repositories.
- **Staging First, Always:** Validate all DDL commands in a sandbox or staging environment before applying them in production. This allows you to detect syntax errors, discover dependency issues, and measure performance impacts. Use representative datasets in staging environments to better mimic real-world results. Some DDL changes (e.g., adding indexes or constraints) can lock tables or cause downtime, so test for duration and locking effects. Maintain CI/CD pipelines that automatically apply and validate migrations on test branches.
- **Enforce Naming Conventions:** Adopt and enforce consistent naming patterns for tables, columns, indexes, constraints, and schemas. Predictable naming improves readability, lowers onboarding

time for new developers, and avoids naming collisions. Consider using prefixes for foreign keys (e.g., fk_user_id) and indexes (e.g., idx_last_name). Avoid reserved words and special characters. Document naming rules as part of your team's SQL style guide.

- **Minimize Downtime:** Schedule DDL changes during low-traffic periods, especially when altering large tables or adding constraints. Use tools like Percona's pt-online-schema-change or native ALGORITHM=INPLACE options to reduce locking. Monitor performance and lock wait times during schema changes. Notify stakeholders before high-risk structural deployments. Consider blue-green or shadow table strategies for zero-downtime migrations.
- **Keep Schemas Lean and Modular:** Resist the urge to over-normalize or include unused fields "just in case." Keep tables clean and normalized to third normal form (3NF), unless denormalization serves a specific performance goal. Modularize schema logic by grouping related objects into logical schemas or using schema namespaces if supported. Small, well-defined tables are easier to maintain and migrate. Remove unused indexes and columns as part of regular schema hygiene.
- **Document Dependencies:** Before applying DDL changes, analyze dependencies like views, stored procedures, triggers, and foreign key constraints. Dropping or altering a table may break downstream logic. Use tools or scripts to trace dependencies. Maintain a data dictionary or ER diagram to visualize relationships. In some systems, metadata tables can be queried to check for dependencies programmatically.
- **Audit DDL Changes:** In production environments, enable audit logging or triggers that record DDL activities. Knowing who changed what and when is crucial for security, compliance, and debugging. Many RDBMSs support general logs, error logs, and custom DDL triggers. Store logs in tamper-proof formats. Consider integrating with monitoring dashboards to alert on unexpected schema changes.

End-of-Chapter Humor

Why did the table get kicked out of the database party? Because it had too many DROP issues and couldn't commit!

Why did the SQL developer go broke? Because they kept rolling back every transaction!

Why don't databases ever get invited to comedy shows? Because they can never handle too many joins—they always crash from laughter!

Conclusion

DDL gives you the tools to architect your database with intention and clarity. It allows you to lay the groundwork for efficient, reliable data storage. Understanding DDL is essential for database professionals who want to take control of their data environments. In the next chapter, we'll move from structure to action and explore how to manipulate that data using DML.

5. DML

Introduction

Data Manipulation Language (DML) is the hands-on portion of SQL. It's where your interaction with the database becomes dynamic and operational. While Data Definition Language (DDL) establishes the architectural framework—the tables, schemas, and constraints—DML is what fills those structures with actual, living data. Think of DDL as building a house and DML as moving in furniture, appliances, and people. Without DML, your database would be little more than an empty shell.

DML includes the essential commands that allow users and applications to create, update, and remove the data within database tables. These commands—INSERT, UPDATE, DELETE, and sometimes even MERGE—enable the day-to-day operations of everything from e-commerce websites to airline booking systems. Whether you're inserting a new customer record, adjusting an inventory count, or purging outdated logs, DML is how you interact with the data layer of your system in real time.

Because DML commands change the actual content of your database, they are almost always used in conjunction with transaction control (TCL) commands such as COMMIT and ROLLBACK. This ensures that critical data modifications can be made reliably and safely, even in the face of network interruptions or application errors. Understanding the behavior of DML statements, their side effects, and their interaction with indexes, triggers, and constraints is essential for both performance and data integrity.

Mastering DML is a foundational skill for anyone working with databases. Whether you're building applications, running analytics, or maintaining production systems, you will use DML more frequently than any other part of SQL. It is the heartbeat of data-driven applications—the part of the language that lets your programs, reports, and users create meaningful, real-world impact from the abstract structure of a relational model.

Core DML Commands

Data Manipulation Language (DML) consists of three fundamental SQL commands that allow users to interact with the data stored in relational database tables:

- INSERT – Adds new data into a table. This is how you populate your database with real-world values, whether it's customer names, product inventory, or transaction records.
- UPDATE – Modifies existing data in a table. Used to correct, adjust, or augment values, this command is essential for reflecting real-time changes like price updates or address changes.
- DELETE – Removes data from a table. This can be used for cleaning up outdated, irrelevant, or erroneous records, but must be used with care to avoid unintentional loss.

Each of these commands can operate on one row, multiple rows, or even the entire table depending on how they're structured. The power—and danger—of DML lies in its flexibility. For example, a simple mistake like omitting a WHERE clause in an UPDATE or DELETE statement can lead to every record in the table being modified or erased. For this reason, it's best practice to develop and test DML queries in staging environments before executing them in production.

Let's consider the implications of each:

INSERT

The INSERT command allows you to add new rows to a table. You must specify the target table and, optionally, the columns and values you wish to add. Here's a typical example:

```
INSERT INTO employees
(name, department, salary)
VALUES ('Alice Chen',
'Marketing', 60000.00);
```

This command adds a new employee record with name, department, and salary values. If your table has constraints (such as NOT NULL, UNIQUE, or CHECK), violating them will raise an error and the row will not be inserted.

You can also insert multiple rows at once:

```
INSERT INTO employees (name, department, salary)
VALUES
('Bob Stone', 'Engineering', 75000.00),
('Clara Yu', 'Design', 68000.00);
```

This saves round trips to the server and enhances performance in bulk-loading scenarios. It is important to make sure that inserted values match the column types and comply with foreign key constraints, if any.

UPDATE

The UPDATE command changes data in existing rows. Without a WHERE clause, all rows will be updated. Consider this example:

```
UPDATE employees
SET salary = salary * 1.10
WHERE department = 'Engineering';
```

Here, all employees in the Engineering department receive a 10% raise. Notice how the WHERE clause helps limit the update scope to only the intended records.

You can update multiple columns simultaneously:

```
UPDATE employees
SET department = 'Operations', salary
= salary + 2000
WHERE name = 'Alice Chen';
```

Be cautious when using subqueries inside updates, as performance can degrade on large datasets. Also, remember that updates trigger changes in indexes and can activate triggers or constraints—so their effects might cascade through the schema.

DELETE

The DELETE command removes rows from a table. Like UPDATE, the DELETE command must be paired with a WHERE clause to avoid unintended data loss.

```
DELETE FROM employees
WHERE hire_date < '2010-01-01';
```

This command removes employees hired before January 1, 2010. If you omit the WHERE clause:

```
DELETE FROM employees;
```

You will delete every record in the employees table—effectively wiping it clean. In systems that lack transactional support or where AUTOCOMMIT is enabled, this operation is irreversible unless backups exist.

DELETE differs from TRUNCATE in that it logs each deleted row (if logging is enabled), can be rolled back, and may activate triggers. TRUNCATE, by contrast, is more efficient but irreversible in most engines.

DML with Transactions

Many DML commands are used within transactions to protect against partial or erroneous changes. A typical transactional sequence looks like this:

```
START TRANSACTION;
UPDATE accounts SET balance
= balance - 100 WHERE id = 1;
UPDATE accounts SET balance
= balance + 100 WHERE id = 2;
COMMIT;
```

This two-step transfer process ensures both updates happen as a unit. If any error occurs, you can use ROLLBACK to undo the changes.

```
START TRANSACTION;
DELETE FROM employees
WHERE department = 'Closed Division';
ROLLBACK;—if you change
your mind or detect an error
```

Transactions allow you to group multiple DML operations together into a single atomic block. This ensures either all changes are committed or none are—critical for financial applications, auditing, or consistency across tables.

Safety Tips

- Always test DML queries on a subset of data or a staging database before deploying to production.
- Use WHERE clauses wisely. Without them, UPDATE and DELETE affect all rows.
- Wrap critical DML commands in transactions to enable rollback if needed.
- Avoid running DML during peak usage hours unless necessary; updates and deletes can lock rows or even full tables.

- Create triggers and constraints to enforce business rules and ensure that DML changes remain within expected bounds.
- Monitor DML performance on large datasets, as poorly designed queries can cause locking, blocking, and timeouts.
- Use parameterized queries in application code to avoid SQL injection and ensure safe handling of user input.
- Maintain audit logs or triggers for sensitive tables to track when and how changes are made.

Summary

DML is the operational muscle of SQL—responsible for the everyday tasks of creating, modifying, and deleting data. Because of its power, it must be used with precision and discipline. By mastering DML and combining it with proper indexing, transaction control, and safety measures, you can ensure your applications remain fast, reliable, and secure. Whether you're processing millions of rows or inserting one customer at a time, DML is your interface to the lifeblood of any database: its data.

INSERT: Adding Data

The INSERT INTO statement is used to add one or more new rows into a table. It is the primary method by which new data enters your database. This operation must align with the table's structure, including mandatory fields, data types, and constraints like NOT NULL or UNIQUE.

Basic Example

```
INSERT INTO books (title, author, published_year)
   VALUES ('The Alchemist',
   'Paulo Coelho',
   1988);
```

This inserts a single row into the books table, adding details about a particular title. The order of the values must match the order of the columns listed.

Multiple Row Insertions

You can insert multiple rows at once by comma-separating VALUES blocks. This is often more efficient than issuing separate INSERT commands.

```
INSERT INTO books (title, author, published_year)
VALUES
('1984', 'George Orwell', 1949),
('Sapiens', 'Yuval Noah Harari', 2011);
```

In bulk data imports, this approach greatly reduces overhead and improves performance.

Default Values and Auto-Increment Fields

You must specify values for all required (non-NULL) fields unless default values are defined. For columns with auto-increment properties (like primary keys), you can omit the field entirely:

```
INSERT INTO books (title, author, published_year)
VALUES ('Brave New World', 'Aldous Huxley', 1932);
```

If the id column is auto-incremented, it will automatically assign the next integer value.

INSERT with SELECT

You can also populate a table with data derived from a query using INSERT INTO ... SELECT:

```
INSERT INTO archived_books
(title, author, published_year)
SELECT title, author, published_year
FROM books
WHERE published_year < 1950;
```

This copies rows from one table to another based on a condition—useful in archiving or history tables.

UPDATE: Editing Data

The UPDATE statement is used to modify existing data. Always include a WHERE clause unless you intend to apply changes to every row. Omitting it can lead to catastrophic overwrites.

Basic Example

```
UPDATE books
    SET published_year = 1989
    WHERE title = 'The Alchemist';
```

This changes the publication year of a single book entry.

Multiple Column Updates

You can update more than one field at once in a single SET clause:

```
UPDATE books
SET author = 'Orwell', published_year = 1950
WHERE title = '1984';
```

Conditional Updates

Updates can include complex logic using subqueries or calculated fields:

```
UPDATE books
SET published_year
= published_year + 1
WHERE author
= 'Yuval Noah Harari';
```

Or use data from other tables:

```
UPDATE books
SET published_year = (
SELECT MIN(published_year)
FROM editions
WHERE editions.book_id
= books.id
)
WHERE EXISTS (
SELECT 1
FROM editions
WHERE editions.book_id
= books.id
);
```

DELETE: Removing Data

The DELETE FROM statement removes rows from a table. It supports the use of WHERE clauses, joins, and subqueries for precision.

Basic Example

```
DELETE FROM books
    WHERE title = 'Sapiens';
```

This removes the row containing that exact title.

Mass Deletes

Be very careful with wide-scope deletions:

```
DELETE FROM books;
```

This deletes every row in the table. In production environments, such operations should always be preceded by a backup or wrapped in a transaction.

DELETE with Joins

You can delete rows based on conditions in other tables:

```
DELETE books
FROM books
JOIN authors ON books.author = authors.name
WHERE authors.country = 'Unknown';
```

This deletes books by authors whose country is unknown—an example of cross-table criteria.

Best Practices for DML

- **Always back up your data** before running mass UPDATE or DELETE commands. Even better, test queries in a staging environment.
- **Use SELECT to preview your WHERE clause.** A simple SELECT * FROM table WHERE ... lets you confirm the rows targeted by your DML query.
- **Use transactions to protect against partial failure.** Wrap risky changes in:
- START TRANSACTION;
- —your DML

COMMIT;

Or use ROLLBACK if anything goes wrong.

- **Use LIMIT clauses** to constrain bulk DML actions for safety and performance:
- DELETE FROM logs ORDER

BY created_at ASC LIMIT 1000;

- **Log DML actions in production**—either through application-layer logging, triggers, or binary logs (if supported). This helps with audits, debugging, and rollback.
- **Avoid user-facing DML from UI inputs unless sanitized.** Use prepared statements to avoid SQL injection.
- **Keep referential integrity in mind.** Deleting or updating a parent record might cascade to child records—check your foreign key constraints and cascading rules.
- **Don't assume defaults.** If a table has DEFAULT values, know what they are before omitting columns from INSERT.

Conclusion

DML is the core of everyday SQL usage. It allows us to add, refine, and delete information, powering everything from dynamic websites to enterprise applications. Mastery of DML enables precise and efficient data control. Once comfortable with DML, you can interact meaningfully with virtually any database. In the next chapter, we'll examine how to regulate access to data using SQL's security toolkit: Data Control Language (DCL).

End-of-Chapter Humor

What happens when a SQL developer gets dumped?

DELETE FROM relationships WHERE status = 'complicated';

Why did the DBA bring a ladder to work?

Because they heard the database had too many levels of abstraction.

Why don't SQL developers like going to the gym?

Because they hate dealing with too many joins.

Why did the query break up with the database table?

It lost interest after too many NULL conversations.

What's a SQL developer's favorite pickup line?

SELECT FROM your_heart WHERE feelings = 'mutual';

Why was the primary key so arrogant?

Because it knew it was unique.

What did the table say to the column who wouldn't stop talking?

"You need a constraint on that mouth!"

Why was the SQL statement unhappy?

Because it couldn't find a good WHERE clause for its life.

Why did the junior developer cry during the meeting?

They used DELETE without a WHERE clause... and it hit them all at once.

When the database was full of bugs, what did the DBA do?

ROLLBACK to a happier time.

6. DQL

Introduction

Data Query Language (DQL) forms the heart of SQL's ability to retrieve, filter, and interpret information from structured datasets. While other sublanguages like DDL and DML provide the foundation and mechanics for building and modifying a database, it is DQL—particularly the SELECT statement—that turns data into insight. DQL allows users to slice, filter, aggregate, and sort data with remarkable precision, enabling complex analytical tasks as well as simple lookups. Whether you're retrieving an individual user profile or generating financial reports spanning billions of rows, the SELECT statement is your primary interface to understanding what's inside the database.

DQL operates on the idea that questions can be formalized into structured syntax. This structure allows humans and machines alike to ask meaningful queries, compare results over time, and extract hidden patterns from data that might otherwise remain buried. SELECT is not just about displaying data—it's about refining and shaping the answer to a specific business, scientific, or operational question. A well-crafted query can reveal trends, surface anomalies, and support strategic decision-making.

The power of DQL comes not just from SELECT itself but from its many companions. Clauses like WHERE allow filtering for precision. ORDER BY helps sort results, while GROUP BY and HAVING enable aggregation and conditional summarization. LIMIT and OFFSET provide pagination and result control. Together, these extensions transform SELECT from a simple data fetcher into a sophisticated analytical engine.

In this chapter, we will explore these tools in depth. You'll learn how to construct effective queries that pull just the data you need, no more and no less. We'll cover core syntax and advanced capabilities like filtering ranges, joining aggregated results, conditional aggregation, and nested subqueries. By the end, you will not only know how to query data—you'll be able to interrogate it fluently, extracting both facts and patterns that lead to insight.

Absolutely. Here is a **quadrupled expansion** of each of the requested sections:

The SELECT Statement

The SELECT command is the cornerstone of Data Query Language (DQL). It enables you to retrieve specific columns or entire rows from a database table. You can use it for everything from simple queries to complex analytics across multiple tables. The basic syntax specifies which columns to return and from which table:

```
SELECT column1, column2, ...
FROM table\_name;
```

If you want to retrieve all the columns from a table, you can use the asterisk wildcard:

```
SELECT * FROM employees;
```

This is convenient for exploration or quick debugging. However, using SELECT in production queries is discouraged for performance and maintainability reasons. Specifying only the columns you need ensures efficient data retrieval, especially in tables with many fields or large volumes of data.

You can also perform expressions inside the SELECT clause, such as mathematical operations or concatenation:

```
SELECT name, salary \* 1.10 AS increased\_salary
FROM employees;
```

And even literal values:

```
SELECT 'Welcome to the Company'
AS message, NOW() AS today;
```

Filtering with WHERE

The WHERE clause filters rows from the result set before any aggregation or sorting occurs. It allows you to focus on specific data that meets given criteria. Here's a basic example:

```
SELECT name, salary
FROM employees
WHERE department = 'Engineering';
```

You can compare values using operators like =, >, <, >=, <=, and !=. Logical operators such as AND, OR, and NOT help combine conditions:

```
SELECT \* FROM employees
WHERE salary > 60000 AND department = 'Sales';
```

You can use IN for membership testing:

```
SELECT \* FROM employees
```

```
WHERE department IN ('Sales',
'Marketing', 'Support');
```

And BETWEEN for range queries:

```
SELECT \* FROM employees
WHERE hire\_date
BETWEEN '2020-01-01'
AND '2023-12-31';
```

Pattern matching with LIKE is also powerful:

```
SELECT \* FROM employees
WHERE name
LIKE 'A%'; —Names starting with A
```

Sorting with ORDER BY

The ORDER BY clause is used to sort query results based on one or more columns. It supports both ascending (ASC) and descending (DESC) order:

```
SELECT name, salary
FROM employees
ORDER BY salary DESC;
```

You can sort by multiple columns for more refined control:

```
SELECT name, department, salary
FROM employees
ORDER BY department ASC, salary DESC;
```

You can even use column position in the ORDER BY clause:

```
SELECT name, salary
FROM employees
ORDER BY 2 DESC;
—Refers to the second column: salary
```

Sorting is evaluated after filtering but before limits or pagination. Proper indexing of sorted columns can significantly improve performance in large datasets.

Grouping with GROUP BY

The GROUP BY clause is used to group rows that share the same value in one or more columns. It's most often paired with aggregate functions like SUM, COUNT, AVG, MIN, and MAX:

```
SELECT department, AVG(salary)
FROM employees
GROUP BY department;
```

You can group by multiple columns for multidimensional aggregations:

```
SELECT department, job\_title, COUNT(\*)
FROM employees
GROUP BY department, job\_title;
```

Using aliases can make the result set more readable:

```
SELECT department,
COUNT(\*) AS employee\_count
FROM employees
GROUP BY department;
```

Note: When using GROUP BY, all selected columns must either appear in the GROUP BY clause or be used in an aggregate function.

Filtering Groups with HAVING

The HAVING clause is used to filter groups created by the GROUP BY clause. It behaves similarly to WHERE, but it operates on aggregated data:

```
SELECT department,
AVG(salary) AS avg\_salary
FROM employees
GROUP BY department
HAVING AVG(salary) > 70000;
```

Unlike WHERE, you can't use column aliases in HAVING in all DBMSs. Use full expressions for portability:

```
SELECT department, COUNT(*)
AS num\_employees
FROM employees
GROUP BY department
HAVING COUNT(*) BETWEEN 5 AND 10;
```

HAVING is evaluated after GROUP BY and before ORDER BY, making it ideal for filtering out insignificant groups from your analysis.

Limiting Results with LIMIT

The LIMIT clause restricts how many rows the query returns. It is extremely useful when previewing large datasets or paginating results:

```
SELECT \* FROM employees
LIMIT 5;
```

To retrieve rows from a specific offset, use the two-parameter form:

```
SELECT \* FROM employees
LIMIT 10 OFFSET 20;
```

This skips the first 20 records and returns the next 10. Some dialects like SQL Server use TOP or FETCH NEXT instead of LIMIT.

Combining ORDER BY and LIMIT gives powerful control over which data appears first:

```
SELECT name, salary
FROM employees
ORDER BY salary DESC
LIMIT 3;
```

This returns the top 3 highest-paid employees.

Combining It All

You can build powerful queries by combining multiple DQL clauses. Here's an advanced example:

```
SELECT department, COUNT(*) AS headcount
FROM employees
WHERE is\_active = TRUE
AND hire\_date >= '2022-01-01'
GROUP BY department
HAVING COUNT(*) > 3
ORDER BY headcount DESC
LIMIT 10;
```

This query does the following:

- Filters only active employees hired after January 1, 2022.
- Groups them by department.
- Filters to only departments with more than 3 employees.
- Sorts the departments by size, largest first.
- Returns the top 10 results.

Understanding how each component fits into the logical query processing order helps you troubleshoot and optimize queries:

1. FROM
2. WHERE
3. GROUP BY
4. HAVING
5. SELECT

6. ORDER BY
7. LIMIT

Selecting from Multiple Tables with Qualified Names

When your query involves multiple tables—such as during joins or subqueries—you often need to refer to specific columns that may share the same name across tables. SQL allows you to qualify each column with its table name to avoid ambiguity. This is done using the dot notation:

```
SELECT table1.costs, table2.size
FROM table1
JOIN table2 ON table1.id = table2.id;
```

In this example, both table1 and table2 may have columns named id, costs, or size, but you're specifying exactly which table each column should be pulled from. This clarity becomes essential in complex joins, especially in databases with standardized naming conventions (like created_at, id, etc.).

You can also use table aliases to shorten your queries while keeping them readable:

```
SELECT t1.costs, t2.size
FROM table1 AS t1
JOIN table2 AS t2 ON t1.id = t2.id;
```

Aliases (t1, t2) act as shorthand and are particularly useful in queries with more than two tables, improving both readability and maintainability.

Being explicit with your table references prevents logic errors and ensures your queries remain understandable as your schema grows in complexity.

Using Fully Qualified Column Names from Multiple Tables

Making the Most of SELECT: Do's and Don'ts

The SELECT statement is one of the most powerful tools in SQL—but with great power comes great responsibility. Efficient and clear queries can dramatically improve performance and maintainability, while careless ones can bog down your database or produce misleading results.

Do's

- **Use specific column names.** Avoid SELECT * in production queries. It may retrieve unnecessary data, slow performance, and break downstream apps when schemas change.
- **Alias your columns for clarity.** Use AS to rename columns, especially for aggregates or when using joins.
- **Use WHERE clauses to limit scope.** Filtering early reduces the amount of data processed and returned.
- **Apply LIMIT when testing.** This protects you from accidentally retrieving millions of rows.
- **Write readable SQL.** Use line breaks and indentation for each clause (SELECT, FROM, WHERE, GROUP BY, etc.) to make queries easier to debug.

- **Leverage indexes smartly.** Queries that filter or join on indexed columns will generally run faster.
- **Use fully qualified names in joins.** When working across multiple tables, use table.column to avoid ambiguity and improve readability.

Don'ts

- **Don't use SELECT * indiscriminately.** It pulls all columns—even those you don't need—wasting memory and bandwidth.
- **Don't forget the WHERE clause.** Accidental full-table scans or deletions often result from omitting conditions.
- **Don't rely on implicit joins.** Use explicit JOIN ... ON syntax for clarity and control.
- **Don't ignore nulls.** Always consider how NULL values will affect your logic in filters and aggregations.
- **Don't overuse nested subqueries.** They can often be replaced with more efficient JOIN or WITH clauses (common table expressions).
- **Don't select unnecessary rows.** Even if you don't store the results, the database still spends time processing them.

In short: be deliberate with your queries. Precision and performance go hand in hand in SQL, and the SELECT statement is where that principle matters most.

Conclusion

DQL empowers you to uncover insights from data using concise and expressive commands. From basic lookups to advanced aggregation and filtering, the SELECT statement and its allies form the backbone of every data analyst's SQL skill set. Mastering these tools turns your database into a responsive, flexible engine for decision-making. In the next chapter, we shift from reading data to controlling access and security: welcome to Data Control Language.

End-of-Chapter Humor

Why did the database administrator go broke? Because he lost his SELECT few clients!

SQL pickup line: "You must be a query, because you've got me SELECTing all day."

7. Joins and Subqueries

Introduction

In relational databases, data is frequently normalized to eliminate redundancy and promote data integrity. This normalization means data is distributed across multiple tables, each focused on a specific entity or relationship. While this structure enhances organization and consistency, it also means that meaningful analysis often requires data to be pulled together from multiple places.

To do this effectively, SQL provides two powerful tools: **joins** and **subqueries**. Joins allow you to combine records from different tables based on shared values in their columns, enabling horizontal integration of data. Subqueries, on the other hand, enable vertical nesting of queries within queries, providing the flexibility to filter, transform, or compute values contextually.

Whether you need to show every order with its corresponding customer details, find employees who earn more than the average salary in their department, or compare cross-tabulated metrics across tables, joins and subqueries are your best allies. This chapter will delve deep into the logic, syntax, performance considerations, and practical use cases of both. Mastering these tools will equip you to answer complex business questions and architect robust data solutions.

Joins

A JOIN clause is used to combine rows from two or more tables based on a related column between them. This mechanism allows you to perform relational operations—bringing together data that belongs together logically, even if it lives in separate tables physically. Joins can be executed between multiple tables in cascading or chained fashion, and often form the backbone of sophisticated reporting.

Types of Joins

- **INNER JOIN** Returns only the rows that have matching values in both tables. It's the most commonly used join, ideal for tightly coupled records.

- **LEFT JOIN (or LEFT OUTER JOIN)** Retrieves all rows from the left table and the matched rows from the right table. Rows from the left table with no match will have NULL values from the right table.
- **RIGHT JOIN (or RIGHT OUTER JOIN)** Retrieves all rows from the right table and the matched rows from the left table. NULLs will fill in where no match exists.
- **FULL OUTER JOIN** Combines the effects of LEFT JOIN and RIGHT JOIN, returning all rows from both tables with NULLs in non-matching rows. Note: MySQL requires a workaround since it doesn't support this join directly.
- **CROSS JOIN** Returns the Cartesian product of both tables. Useful for generating all combinations, such as product-price matrices or schedule grids.
- **SELF JOIN** A table is joined with itself. Useful for hierarchical queries like employee-manager relationships.

Each join type serves a particular purpose and is most effective when paired with clear relational logic and indexes.

Join Example: INNER JOIN

Suppose you have two tables: customers and orders. To find each customer's order history, you can write:

```
SELECT customers.name, orders.order_date
FROM customers
INNER JOIN orders
ON customers.id = orders.customer_id;
```

This query links customers with their orders via the shared id field, displaying only those with successful matches in both tables.

Aliasing in Joins

Aliases simplify SQL syntax, especially in joins involving many columns and long table names. Aliasing improves readability and conciseness:

```
SELECT c.name, o.order_date
```

```
FROM customers AS c
JOIN orders AS o
ON c.id = o.customer_id;
```

Here, c and o are table aliases that save typing and make the logic clearer. This practice is especially useful when joining more than two tables or when dealing with subqueries embedded in joins.

You can also alias columns for clarity:

```
SELECT c.name AS customer_name, o.order_date AS date
FROM customers AS c
JOIN orders AS o ON c.id = o.customer_id;
```

By doing so, result sets become more understandable, especially in BI dashboards or exportable reports.

Subqueries

Subqueries, also referred to as nested queries or inner queries, are essential tools in SQL for structuring modular, layered logic within a single statement. These queries are embedded inside another SQL query and can appear in various clauses such as exttttSELECT, exttttFROM, and exttttWHERE. Subqueries are especially powerful for filtering datasets, performing calculated comparisons, computing aggregates on-the-fly, and supplying values for outer queries without explicitly joining tables. They enable more expressive queries and help in decomposing complex logic into understandable steps.

A subquery can return a single value (scalar), a single column (list), or a table (multiple rows and columns). They can be correlated (referencing the outer query) or uncorrelated (independent of the outer query). Understanding when and how to use subqueries enhances your ability to answer business questions with elegance and precision.

Subquery in WHERE Clause

A subquery in the exttttWHERE clause is commonly used for filtering a result set based on values from another table:

```
SELECT name
FROM customers
WHERE id IN (
SELECT customer_id
FROM orders
WHERE total > 100
```

```
);
```

This example returns the names of customers who have placed at least one order with a total value greater than 100. The inner query generates a list of qualifying customer IDs, which is then used by the outer query to filter the extttcustomers table.

You can also use extttEXISTS to test whether the subquery returns any result:

```
SELECT name
FROM customers c
WHERE EXISTS (
SELECT 1 FROM orders o
WHERE o.customer_id = c.id AND o.total > 100
);
```

This correlated subquery checks for the existence of any qualifying order per customer.

Subquery in FROM Clause (Derived Table)

Subqueries used in the extttFROM clause act like temporary tables (known as derived tables or inline views):

```
SELECT avg_order
FROM (
SELECT customer_id, AVG(total) AS avg_order
FROM orders
GROUP BY customer_id
) AS sub;
```

This query calculates the average order total for each customer within the subquery and then returns those averages from the outer query.

You can also perform joins on derived tables:

```
SELECT c.name, s.avg_order
FROM customers c
JOIN (
SELECT customer_id, AVG(total) AS avg_order
FROM orders
GROUP BY customer_id
) s ON c.id = s.customer_id;
```

Here, we enrich customer information with calculated order averages using a subquery joined to the extttcustomers table.

Subquery in SELECT Clause

You can embed subqueries inside the extttSELECT clause to return scalar values per row:

```
SELECT name,
(
SELECT COUNT(*)
FROM orders
WHERE orders.customer_id = customers.id
) AS order_count
FROM customers;
```

This correlated subquery counts how many orders each customer has placed. It's a compact alternative to using joins and extttGROUP BY.

Another example is calculating latest order date:

```
SELECT name,
(
SELECT MAX(order_date)
FROM orders
WHERE orders.customer_id = customers.id
) AS last_order
FROM customers;
```

This shows each customer's most recent order date using a scalar subquery in the projection list.

Combining Joins and Subqueries

Subqueries and joins are not mutually exclusive—in fact, many real-world problems require both. You can use subqueries to pre-filter data, aggregate results, or isolate special logic before performing a join.

```
SELECT c.name, o.total
FROM customers c
JOIN (
SELECT *
FROM orders
WHERE total > 100
) o ON c.id = o.customer_id;
```

This example uses a subquery to filter for high-value orders, then joins that result with the customer table.

Another common pattern is filtering joins based on aggregate values:

```
SELECT c.name, s.total_orders
FROM customers c
```

```
JOIN (
SELECT customer_id, COUNT(*) AS total_orders
FROM orders
GROUP BY customer_id
HAVING COUNT(*) > 5
) s ON c.id = s.customer_id;
```

This query finds customers who have placed more than five orders.

When to Use Joins vs. Subqueries

- Use **joins** when you need to combine data from multiple tables side by side—e.g., merging customers and their orders.
- Use **subqueries** when you need to filter or transform data before combining—e.g., computing aggregates or isolating complex filters.
- **Joins** tend to be more performant for large result sets and are easier to index and optimize.
- **Subqueries** can enhance modularity, simplify nested logic, and make queries easier to understand in certain scenarios.
- Consider readability and maintainability—use subqueries to isolate calculations or logic when a direct join would become too complex.
- Avoid deeply nested or correlated subqueries in performance-critical applications; use CTEs or materialized views where appropriate.

With thoughtful design, both joins and subqueries become indispensable allies in solving analytical and operational database challenges.

Best Practices: Do's and Don'ts of Joins and Subqueries

Writing optimized SQL requires more than just functional correctness. Poorly written joins or subqueries can drastically slow performance or even cause memory exhaustion in large-scale systems. This section outlines the strategic **do's and don'ts** of using joins and subqueries for performance, clarity, and maintainability.

Do's

- **DO use explicit JOIN syntax instead of comma-separated tables.** This improves clarity and reduces logical errors.
- —Preferred
- SELECT c.name, o.total
- FROM customers c

JOIN orders o ON c.id = o.customer_id;

- **DO filter early using WHERE or ON conditions.** This minimizes the number of rows being joined or passed to subqueries.
- SELECT c.name, o.total
- FROM customers c
- JOIN orders o ON c.id = o.customer_id

WHERE o.total > 100;

- **DO index the columns used in joins and subquery filters.** Especially on foreign keys and primary keys to speed up matching and lookup.
- **DO use derived tables (subqueries in the FROM clause) to pre-aggregate large datasets.**
- SELECT region, AVG(avg_order)
- AS regional_avg
- FROM (
- SELECT region, customer_id,
- AVG(total) AS avg_order
- FROM orders
- GROUP BY region,
- customer_id
-) AS sub

GROUP BY region;

- **DO analyze your execution plan.** Use EXPLAIN or EXPLAIN

ANALYZE to see if your query is using indexes or executing unnecessary full table scans.

- **DO normalize for storage, then denormalize selectively for performance.** Denormalizing avoids deep join chains for read-heavy workloads.
- **DO test on realistic data sizes.** A query may seem fast on test data but degrade badly on production-scale datasets.
- **DO name your derived tables and subqueries with clear aliases.** It improves readability and helps debugging.

Don'ts

- **DON'T use SELECT * in joins.** It fetches unnecessary columns and increases memory usage. Specify only needed fields.
- **DON'T nest subqueries unnecessarily.** Each layer adds complexity and can slow down execution.
- —Inefficient
- SELECT name
- FROM customers
- WHERE id IN (
- SELECT customer_id
- FROM orders
- WHERE customer_id IN (
- SELECT id FROM blacklist
-)

);

- **DON'T join huge tables without filtering.** Unfiltered joins can create massive intermediate results (Cartesian products), slowing performance dramatically.
- **DON'T assume subqueries always perform worse than joins.** In some cases—especially for filtering—subqueries can outperform joins depending on indexes and execution plans.
- **DON'T forget to test for NULLs in LEFT JOINs.** Unexpected

NULLs can break logic if not handled explicitly.

- SELECT c.name, o.total
- FROM customers c
- LEFT JOIN orders o ON c.id = o.customer_id

WHERE o.total IS NULL;

- **DON'T use correlated subqueries inside SELECT or WHERE unless necessary.** They execute once per row, leading to serious inefficiency in large datasets.
- **DON'T assume database engines optimize your query the way you think.** Always verify with execution plans or profiling tools.

When used wisely, joins and subqueries can answer complex business questions efficiently and elegantly. But without proper care, they can become the main bottleneck in database performance. Practicing the above do's and avoiding the common pitfalls will keep your SQL effective, maintainable, and performant at scale.

Conclusion

Joins and subqueries are essential tools for any SQL user. Joins help integrate data across tables, while subqueries allow more modular logic. Understanding how and when to use each makes you a more powerful and flexible query writer. Whether you're answering business questions, generating reports, or powering web applications, these tools are central to relational thinking. Practice both extensively—they will appear in nearly every real-world SQL scenario.

End-of-Chapter Humor

- Why did the SQL query go on a date with a subquery?Because it wanted something nested yet committed.
- Joins are like relationships: INNER is mutual love, LEFT is unrequited love, RIGHT is being loved, and FULL is... complicated.
- I tried to CROSS JOIN my laundry with my dishes—now I just have

wet clothes and soapy plates.

- Subqueries are like dreams inside dreams. Just don't go too many layers deep without backup.

8. TCL

Introduction

Transaction Control Language (TCL) is a crucial component of SQL that ensures the accuracy, consistency, and reliability of data within relational databases. While SQL commands like DDL and DML define or modify data and structure, TCL commands control how and when changes are finalized or undone. When multiple changes must be logically treated as a single operation—such as transferring funds, updating inventory, or registering multiple user actions—TCL enables those operations to be grouped, validated, and either saved or discarded together.

A transaction is more than just a sequence of commands—it's a statement of intent that guarantees safe execution. Without transactions, partial failures (such as one successful UPDATE followed by a failed DELETE) could corrupt data and compromise reliability. TCL makes SQL systems enterprise-ready by allowing developers to define when operations start, succeed, or fail without compromising the database state. This functionality is especially vital in high-stakes environments such as financial systems, inventory tracking, e-commerce, authentication, payroll systems, and healthcare.

By managing transaction flow, SQL becomes a truly resilient and fault-tolerant tool. Through transaction boundaries and control mechanisms, you gain fine-grained control over how changes are processed in concurrent environments, making TCL not just a utility but a safeguard against systemic errors.

Historical Origins of TCL

The concept of Transaction Control Language (TCL) was born out of a fundamental need in computing: ensuring data integrity in the face of uncertainty—be it hardware failure, software crashes, or conflicting user actions. As relational database systems matured in the 1970s and 1980s, developers and database architects recognized that operations involving multiple data changes had to be grouped in such a way that they either succeeded entirely or failed entirely. This need gave rise to the notion of the transaction.

Early Roots in Banking and Business Systems

One of the first domains to demand strict transactional consistency was banking. Consider a simple money transfer: deducting money from one account and adding it to another. If only the first operation succeeds, money disappears; if only the second succeeds, money appears out of thin air. Early COBOL-based systems tried to handle this with procedural logic, but it was error-prone and inflexible.

With the rise of relational database systems like IBM's System R and Oracle in the late 1970s and early 1980s, a formal model for transactions emerged. These systems introduced commands to commit or roll back changes, so that partial updates could be avoided entirely. As a result, transaction control became an integral part of Structured Query Language (SQL) by the time the ANSI SQL-86 standard was formalized.

The ACID Principles

By the mid-1980s, database researchers Jim Gray and Andreas Reuter helped define the theoretical underpinnings of transaction processing through their seminal work, Transaction Processing: Concepts and Techniques. It was in this era that the ACID model (Atomicity, Consistency, Isolation, Durability) crystallized as the gold standard for reliable database behavior.

Each of these principles maps directly to what Transaction Control Language manages:

Atomicity: Managed through BEGIN, COMMIT, and ROLLBACK.

Consistency: Ensured by letting transactions either succeed entirely or not at all.

Isolation: Handled by concurrency control mechanisms behind the scenes.

Durability: Guaranteed once a transaction is committed to disk.

TCL as an Official SQL Category

Although SQL originally focused on querying and defining data (SELECT, CREATE, INSERT), the inclusion of TCL commands made SQL a full-fledged transactional language. Commands like BEGIN, COMMIT, ROLLBACK, and later SAVEPOINT and RELEASE SAVEPOINT, were standardized in SQL:1992 and became critical to enterprise-grade applications.

This expansion allowed developers to confidently design complex workflows—like order processing, payroll systems, or flight bookings—without worrying about partial updates or inconsistent states.

Modern Usage and the Role of TCL Today

Today, TCL is indispensable in any relational database that supports ACID transactions, from MySQL and PostgreSQL to Oracle, SQL Server, and DB2. Whether implemented natively or augmented through application-level transaction managers (such as in Java's JDBC or Python's SQLAlchemy), the principles of TCL remain vital.

Moreover, with the rise of distributed systems and microservices, transaction control has evolved into even more sophisticated models—like distributed two-phase commit and eventual consistency. Still, the core concepts introduced by TCL remain foundational.

In short: Transaction Control Language didn't arise out of luxury—it was a response to real-world failure, complexity, and concurrency. From paper checks to digital ledgers, from mainframes to cloud platforms, TCL continues to be the silent guardian that ensures our data stays whole, consistent, and trustworthy.

What Is a Transaction?

A transaction is a logically grouped series of one or more SQL operations that must all succeed or fail together. This enables safe data manipulation and recovery in the face of application crashes, hardware failure, or user error. Transactions prevent inconsistencies by guaranteeing that each operation respects the atomic contract—it either commits fully or not at all.

Transactions are characterized by the four **ACID** properties:

- **Atomicity** — Guarantees that all operations within the transaction complete successfully or none do. There is no in-between state.
- **Consistency** — Ensures that the database starts and ends in a valid state. Business rules and integrity constraints are never violated.
- **Isolation** — Prevents interference between concurrent transactions. Each one acts as if it were executing in a vacuum.
- **Durability** — Once a transaction is committed, the changes survive system crashes, power failures, or restarts.

These properties protect both users and systems from data anomalies and support concurrent operations without sacrificing correctness.

Key TCL Commands

TCL provides the vocabulary for managing transactions. It defines how transactions begin, succeed, fail, and interact with specific checkpoints.

BEGIN / START TRANSACTION

Starts a new transaction block. Different RDBMSs may use either BEGIN or START TRANSACTION:

```
START TRANSACTION;
—or simply
BEGIN;
```

This marks the point from which all subsequent operations are grouped together as one atomic unit until a COMMIT or ROLLBACK is issued.

COMMIT

Finalizes the transaction. All changes made since the last BEGIN or START TRANSACTION become permanent.

```
COMMIT;
```

Once committed, the changes become visible to other users and are written to disk. This concludes the current transaction block.

ROLLBACK

Cancels the transaction. Any changes made during the current transaction are undone:

```
ROLLBACK;
```

This command is essential when errors occur or if your application logic determines that the transaction should not proceed.

SAVEPOINT

Sets a marker within a transaction that allows partial rollback. Useful in long, complex transactions:

```
SAVEPOINT before_update;
—perform some changes
ROLLBACK TO SAVEPOINT before_update;
```

This provides more granular control within transactions and can reduce the cost of failure.

RELEASE SAVEPOINT

Removes a previously defined savepoint. Once released, it can no longer be rolled back to:

```
RELEASE SAVEPOINT before_update;
```

This helps avoid unnecessary memory use when savepoints are no longer needed.

Transaction Example

Here's a transaction that transfers money between two accounts:

```
START TRANSACTION;
UPDATE accounts SET balance
= balance - 100 WHERE id = 1;
UPDATE accounts SET balance
= balance + 100 WHERE id = 2;
COMMIT;
```

If either update fails, you can issue a ROLLBACK; before COMMIT; to undo both changes and preserve data integrity.

Savepoint Variation:

```
START TRANSACTION;
UPDATE accounts SET balance
```

```
= balance - 100 WHERE id = 1;
SAVEPOINT after_debit;
UPDATE accounts SET balance
= balance + 100 WHERE id = 2;
—Suppose this fails
ROLLBACK TO after_debit;
—Maybe apply alternate logic
COMMIT;
```

Best Practices for Using TCL

- **Test changes before committing:** Always verify updates on staging environments or with SELECT statements before issuing COMMIT.
- **Keep transactions short:** Long transactions can cause deadlocks, timeouts, or row locking conflicts. Break up large batches into smaller, manageable units.
- **Use savepoints wisely:** When writing multi-step logic (like multi-account transfers), insert savepoints after each logical step.
- **Avoid mixing DDL and DML in the same transaction:** Some RDBMSs treat DDL as auto-committed. Mixing it with data manipulation could break transactional guarantees.
- **Implement error handling logic:** In application code, wrap SQL calls in error traps so that a failed operation triggers a rollback.
- **Profile and monitor performance:** Use execution plans, logs, or profiling tools to measure transaction duration, lock contention, and throughput.
- **Use isolation levels appropriately:** Know your options: READ COMMITTED, REPEATABLE READ, SERIALIZABLE, etc. Choose based on consistency vs. concurrency trade-offs.
- **Log all transactional events:** Especially in financial or security-sensitive systems, maintain audit logs to record what changes were made, when, and by whom.

Do's and Don'ts of TCL

Transaction Control Language (TCL) commands are powerful tools for maintaining data integrity, but they must be used with care. Below are the most important do's and don'ts to follow when working with transactions:

TCL Do's

- **Do use transactions to group logically related operations:** Any sequence of actions that must succeed or fail together—such as transferring money between accounts—should be wrapped in a transaction.
- **Do commit only after verifying success:** Perform all necessary validations, exception checks, or integrity tests before issuing a COMMIT.
- **Do use SAVEPOINTs for long transactions:** Savepoints let you break a transaction into manageable chunks and recover selectively if needed.
- **Do test transactions thoroughly in development and staging:** Even small mistakes in transaction logic can result in data corruption or lost updates.
- **Do keep transactions short and efficient:** The longer a transaction remains open, the more likely it is to cause locking issues, performance bottlenecks, or deadlocks.

TCL Don'ts

- **Don't forget to commit or roll back:** Leaving a transaction open can lock tables or rows indefinitely, blocking other users and creating performance issues.
- **Don't nest transactions unless your DBMS supports it:** Some systems will throw errors or silently flatten nested transactions, potentially causing unexpected results.
- **Don't use ROLLBACK carelessly:** While rollback is a safety mechanism, overuse can hide bugs or make debugging difficult by

wiping changes you need to analyze.

- **Don't wrap all operations in a transaction by default:** Not every query needs transactional control. Unnecessary transactions reduce performance and add complexity.
- **Don't assume atomicity without understanding your DBMS:** Different SQL engines handle transaction isolation and failure differently—study your DBMS documentation for precise behavior.

Summary: TCL provides the backbone for reliable, consistent database operations, but careless use can introduce risks instead of reducing them. Understanding the trade-offs between transactional safety and system performance is essential for writing clean, efficient, and trustworthy SQL.

Conclusion

Transaction Control Language makes SQL resilient and trustworthy. It empowers developers to group changes logically, ensure consistency, and recover gracefully from errors. By mastering TCL commands like COMMIT, ROLLBACK, and SAVEPOINT, you gain fine-grained control over how and when data changes are persisted. Whether you're writing financial software, order systems, or login platforms, TCL offers the reliability your data needs. Transactions aren't just a technical feature—they're your safety net.

End-of-Chapter Humor

Why did the SQL transaction break up with its girlfriend?

- Because she couldn't COMMIT.

What did the database say after a terrible date?

- "Let's ROLLBACK and pretend this never happened."

Why don't SQL transactions ever panic during a crisis?

- Because they always know they can fall back on a SAVEPOINT.

What's an SQL developer's favorite pickup line?

- "You must be a transaction, because you complete me... atomically."

Why was the SQL transaction such a great partner?

- Because it was reliable, isolated, and never left anything uncommitted.

How do SQL developers handle regret?

- They just ROLLBACK and try again.

What did the pessimistic transaction say to the optimistic one?

- "You'll COMMIT to anything."

Why did the DBA lock himself in his office?

- He was experiencing a deadlock with HR.

Knock Knock. **Who's there?** *TCL.* **TCL who?**

- TCL you later... after I COMMIT to this joke.

Relationship Advice from SQL:

- Never trust someone who doesn't honor your SAVEPOINTs.

9. DCL

Introduction

Data Control Language (DCL) is essential for managing who can access and manipulate data within a database system. It allows administrators to grant and revoke user permissions, helping enforce data security and compliance policies. While DCL commands are fewer than those of other SQL sublanguages, their role is critical—ensuring that sensitive information is protected and that database operations are traceable and accountable. Whether you're working with a team or deploying an application, understanding DCL is fundamental to maintaining a secure and controlled environment.

DCL sits at the intersection of SQL and organizational policy. As databases grow more complex and integrated into every aspect of business operations, it's no longer enough to focus on just storing and retrieving data. Controlling who can do what, when, and to which parts of the database is vital. This is where DCL becomes a gatekeeper.

DCL empowers administrators to establish boundaries. It enforces separation of duties, isolates development environments from production data, and ensures that only verified identities can execute sensitive operations. Unlike DML or DDL, which deal with data and structures, DCL manages people. It creates a secure ecosystem where accountability and traceability are guaranteed.

Furthermore, in regulated industries such as healthcare, finance, or government, failure to apply proper DCL policies can result in severe legal penalties. Granting excessive privileges or forgetting to revoke access from former employees poses major risks. In such cases, DCL is not just a technical tool but also a compliance necessity.

In this chapter, we dive into the two principal DCL commands—GRANT and REVOKE—and explore how privileges and roles function across different systems. We'll also look at practical tips and strategies for minimizing security vulnerabilities through structured permission design.

Historical Development of Data Control Language (DCL)

Data Control Language (DCL), while often overshadowed by more frequently used SQL sublanguages like DDL, DML, and DQL, has its roots in the original conception of the relational database and the broader evolution of SQL itself. To understand the origins of DCL, it is necessary to first consider the foundational milestones of relational database systems.

The Birth of the Relational Model and SQL

The relational model was first proposed in 1970 by British computer scientist Edgar F. Codd in his seminal paper, *"A Relational Model of Data for Large Shared Data Banks"*. Codd envisioned a mathematical approach to data storage and retrieval, one based on set theory and first-order predicate logic. This was a radical departure from the hierarchical and network models in use at the time.

Codd's work inspired researchers at IBM to develop the first relational database prototype, called System R, in the mid-1970s. As part of that effort, IBM researchers Donald D. Chamberlin and Raymond F. Boyce created a new query language called SEQUEL (Structured English Query Language), which later evolved into SQL due to a trademark conflict.

SQL (Structured Query Language) quickly became the standard for relational database communication. By 1986, the American National Standards Institute (ANSI) adopted SQL as the official standard query language for relational databases, followed by ISO in 1987. Early versions of the standard—such as SQL-86 and SQL-89—focused primarily on basic querying and data manipulation.

The Emergence of DCL in SQL Standards

As relational databases matured and gained adoption in enterprise environments, the need for granular access control became apparent. Systems now had to manage not just data storage and retrieval, but also the *security* and *authorization* of users accessing that data.

This led to the development of the **Data Control Language (DCL)** subset of SQL, which formalized commands like:

- GRANT – to assign privileges to users or roles
- REVOKE – to remove those privileges

While DCL was not always explicitly demarcated in early SQL standards, its functionality became increasingly prominent starting with **SQL-92**, which incorporated clearer definitions for access control and user privileges. Later SQL standards (SQL:1999, SQL:2003, and beyond) expanded on this by introducing concepts such as roles, access control hierarchies, and authorization identifiers.

DCL in Practice: Vendor-Specific Implementations

Major relational database management systems (RDBMSs) implemented DCL differently:

- **Oracle** supported roles and privilege management early on, allowing separation of system privileges (like CREATE USER) and object privileges (like SELECT on a table).
- **SQL Server** introduced schema-based access control and supported integrated Windows authentication for enterprise environments.
- **MySQL** evolved from basic user management to more sophisticated role-based access control (RBAC) starting in version 8.0.
- **PostgreSQL** maintained strict SQL standard compliance but extended its GRANT/REVOKE model with advanced features such as row-level security and SE-Linux integration.

These variations demonstrate how DCL grew in parallel with industry needs for robust, flexible, and auditable access management.

Modern DCL and the Future of Access Control

In today's data-centric environments, Data Control Language (DCL) has evolved from a simple privilege-management utility into a cornerstone of enterprise-level data security, governance, and compliance strategy. As businesses operate in increasingly distributed, regulated, and high-stakes data landscapes, DCL plays a foundational role in helping organizations safeguard information, enforce access boundaries, and ensure the traceability of every operation.

DCL commands—primarily GRANT and REVOKE—have been dramatically enhanced in modern RDBMS implementations to serve the needs of large-scale, multi-user, and multi-tenant systems. No longer limited to basic permissions, today's DCL is tightly integrated with advanced identity management and policy enforcement mechanisms.

Integration with Identity and Access Management (IAM)

Modern DCL is increasingly embedded within federated identity systems that span cloud and on-premise resources. Platforms like AWS IAM, Azure Active Directory, and Google Cloud IAM connect user identities across services, enabling centralized policy management. RDBMSs often integrate with these systems to map users and roles dynamically, replacing static user definitions with flexible, cloud-native controls. This means DCL doesn't operate in isolation but rather as part of a larger identity strategy, enabling:

- Single Sign-On (SSO) for database services
- Role-based access control (RBAC) mapped to cloud-native roles
- Attribute-based access control (ABAC) using metadata and contextual factors

Encryption, Auditing, and Compliance Enforcement

DCL today must do more than simply restrict access. It often works hand-in-hand with encryption protocols and auditing mechanisms. For instance, in environments governed by regulations such as **HIPAA**, **GDPR**, or **SOX**, DCL enforces compliance by:

- Granting access only to authorized personnel based on purpose and role
- Logging each action, including GRANT/REVOKE events, for forensic audit trails
- Restricting access to encrypted data unless the user possesses the

decryption key
- Enforcing data retention, archival, or redaction policies

In PostgreSQL and Oracle, for example, DCL is supported by extensions and modules for auditing (pgaudit, Oracle Audit Vault) that log privilege changes and query usage.

Fine-Grained Access Control (FGAC)

One of the most important evolutions of DCL is the support for fine-grained access control. Instead of merely granting SELECT or UPDATE on an entire table, administrators can now:

- Limit access to individual columns (column-level permissions)
- Define **row-level security** (RLS), restricting visibility based on data attributes or session context
- Create policies using CREATE POLICY and assign them dynamically using ALTER TABLE ENABLE ROW LEVEL SECURITY

These capabilities are vital in shared environments such as Software-as-a-Service (SaaS), where one table might store customer data for hundreds of tenants. DCL-backed row-level filters ensure that each user only sees data belonging to their organization.

Multi-Tenant and Zero-Trust Environments

The proliferation of multi-tenant architectures and zero-trust security models has pushed DCL to operate in more dynamic, real-time environments. In zero-trust systems, no user is inherently trusted, and every request is verified against policies. DCL helps enforce:

- Session-based access rules based on time, location, and device identity
- Least privilege enforcement across microservices and containerized apps
- Real-time privilege revocation and propagation

Cloud-native databases (e.g., Google Cloud Spanner, AWS Aurora) now support DCL via APIs that dynamically update access privileges in sync with external policy engines like Open Policy Agent (OPA).

Data Mesh, Data Lakes, and DCL Governance

As organizations adopt modern architectures such as **data mesh**, **data lakehouses**, and **fabric-based integration**, DCL must extend beyond traditional SQL systems. In these ecosystems, DCL concepts are applied across distributed storage systems, often using governance layers like Apache Ranger or Azure Purview. These tools allow admins to:

- Define policies once and enforce them across relational and non-relational stores
- Grant SELECT privileges across structured and semi-structured data
- Enforce dynamic masking of sensitive attributes depending on the user's role

This unified governance model brings SQL-based DCL principles into modern data ecosystems that span Spark, Hive, Snowflake, and more.

Future Directions

The future of DCL lies in greater automation, contextual awareness, and integration with DevSecOps pipelines. Key innovations on the horizon include:

- Self-service access request workflows with built-in approvals and audit logging
- AI-assisted privilege recommendation systems that suggest least-privilege configurations
- GitOps-style policy-as-code frameworks that version control and deploy GRANT/REVOKE logic
- Autonomous privilege management engines that respond to behavioral analytics and threat signals

Conclusion

DCL has come a long way from its static roots. In modern ecosystems, it operates as a dynamic, context-aware, and policy-driven mechanism at the intersection of security, governance, and operations. As databases continue to evolve in complexity and scope, DCL will remain a critical guardian—ensuring data is accessed not only efficiently but responsibly, lawfully, and ethically.

Though modest in its command set, DCL embodies one of the most essential purposes of any database system: safeguarding information. Its historical development—emerging from the broader evolution of SQL and relational databases—reflects a maturing understanding of data not just as a resource to be queried, but as an asset to be protected. From humble beginnings to sophisticated role-based ecosystems, DCL has become the backbone of secure, multi-user data environments.

Core DCL Commands

GRANT

The GRANT statement is used to assign specific privileges to database users or roles. These permissions determine what actions a user can perform on objects like tables, views, or procedures.

```
GRANT SELECT,
INSERT ON employees
TO analyst_user;
```

This example gives the user analyst_user permission to query and insert data into the employees table. You can also grant permissions globally or on a database level.

The GRANT command can include clauses such as WITH GRANT OPTION, allowing users to propagate the same permissions to others:

```
GRANT SELECT
ON employees
TO manager_user
WITH GRANT OPTION;
```

REVOKE

The REVOKE statement removes previously granted privileges from a user or role.

```
REVOKE INSERT ON employees
FROM analyst_user;
```

This command takes away the ability of analyst_user to insert data into the employees table while leaving other permissions (like SELECT) intact.

Revoking privileges can also cascade if the user was granted privileges with the GRANT OPTION, affecting other downstream users:

```
REVOKE SELECT ON employees
FROM manager_user;
```

Privileges in Detail

Privileges can be classified as:

- **Object-level privileges:** Permissions like SELECT, INSERT, UPDATE, DELETE, and EXECUTE that apply to specific tables, views, or stored procedures.
- **Administrative privileges:** Permissions such as GRANT OPTION (the ability to grant privileges to others), CREATE USER, and ALTER that apply at the schema or server level.
- **System privileges:** Higher-level capabilities, including starting/stopping servers, managing system configurations, or accessing auditing logs.
- **Role management privileges:** These allow creation, assignment, or revocation of user-defined roles, enabling hierarchical security.

In some systems like MySQL or PostgreSQL, additional privilege granularity exists. You can assign row-level or column-level permissions, or restrict access to certain stored procedures only.

Roles and Best Practices

- **Use roles to group permissions.** Instead of assigning rights individually, create roles like data_analyst, developer, or admin and assign users to those roles. This simplifies onboarding and revocation.

- **Follow the principle of least privilege.** Only grant the minimum permissions necessary for a user to perform their task. Avoid giving broad access like GRANT ALL unless absolutely required.
- **Audit permissions periodically.** Remove outdated users, stale roles, and unused privileges. This reduces exposure to internal or external threats.
- **Avoid using root/admin accounts.** Use fine-grained users for different services or departments, and disable root access where feasible.
- **Document all DCL changes.** Track who changed what, when, and why. Integrate permission management into version control where possible.
- **Use default deny strategies.** Grant access explicitly rather than relying on implicit trust or default permissive settings.

Security Implications

Effective use of DCL enhances the security posture of your system. Improper access control can lead to unauthorized data exposure, accidental data modification, or privilege escalation attacks. Most RDBMSs offer logging and auditing tools to track permission changes and access patterns—utilize them.

DCL is also your first line of defense against SQL injection attacks that exploit elevated permissions. If a low-level user is compromised but only has SELECT access, the impact is much smaller than if they had full INSERT/UPDATE/DELETE capabilities.

In highly secure environments, DCL policies are often reviewed and enforced by separate security teams, not developers. Policies might include:

- **Time-based permissions** – Users granted access for a limited period.
- **Multi-factor access workflows** – Combining DCL with external identity management systems.
- **Access transparency reports** – Allowing users to see what privileges

they hold.

In short, DCL is not just about syntax—it's about strategy, accountability, and trust management in the database world.

Conclusion

Data Control Language (DCL) is the quiet sentinel of SQL—a modest set of commands with outsized influence over the security, integrity, and governance of data. While DCL's syntax is compact, its responsibility is immense: it determines who can read, write, modify, or administrate the data and schema itself. The power of the database rests not just in its ability to store and manipulate data, but in its ability to enforce boundaries—and DCL is the language of those boundaries.

Through commands like GRANT and REVOKE, database administrators are endowed with the tools to construct a secure and well-partitioned data environment. These commands empower organizations to ensure that only authorized users have access to sensitive information or mission-critical operations. This is not merely a matter of best practices—it's a regulatory imperative. In a world governed by GDPR, HIPAA, SOX, PCI-DSS, and similar frameworks, failure to implement robust access control can mean catastrophic legal, financial, and reputational consequences.

Consider the environments where data sovereignty matters most: hospitals, banks, defense systems, academic research labs, legal firms. In each of these settings, DCL ensures that patient data remains private, financial records remain intact, and legal documents remain untampered. The principle of least privilege—giving users only the permissions they need to perform their work, and nothing more—is the philosophical bedrock of modern DCL implementation. It fosters an architecture of trust and accountability, where every user's access is a deliberate choice, not an oversight.

And this architecture is not static. As businesses evolve, team members come and go, applications shift, and new compliance rules emerge, DCL helps maintain order through roles, privilege auditing, and revocation policies. A security-conscious database is not only locked—it is intelligently and adaptively governed.

The evolution of DCL mirrors the growing maturity of SQL and the databases that implement it. Originally conceived when databases were isolated and internal, DCL has grown to support the modern realities of federated cloud systems, zero-trust architectures, and granular row-level access in multi-tenant environments. Whether you're working on an enterprise ERP system, a SaaS product with thousands of users, or a solo side project with minimal access layers, DCL still plays a role. It teaches discipline, foresight, and humility: discipline to grant only what is necessary; foresight to anticipate access escalation risks; and humility to always log and audit changes.

When used properly, DCL enhances collaboration while preserving accountability. Teams can work concurrently on shared data assets without stepping on each other's privileges. Roles can be structured to mirror organizational hierarchies. Administrators can trace any privilege escalation, track breaches, and revoke access in real-time when necessary.

Yet it must be said: with great power comes great responsibility. Granting the wrong privilege to the wrong user, or failing to revoke access after a role change, opens doors to breaches, misuse, or accidental loss. Therefore, DCL should never be treated as an afterthought—it should be built into your schema design, application logic, deployment strategy, and audit routines from the start.

To maximize the power of DCL, remember these parting principles:

- **Design with security in mind.** Build role structures and access strategies as part of your data model—not after.
- **Audit regularly.** Permissions drift over time; periodic audits catch orphaned users and unused access paths.
- **Use roles, not individuals.** Assign privileges to roles and attach users to roles—it scales better and aligns with real-world org charts.
- **Least privilege is best practice.** Always grant the minimal required access, especially in production systems.
- **Never assume safety.** Logs, alerts, and monitoring should accompany every significant permission change.

In sum, DCL is where database administration meets risk management. Its commands may be simple, but their consequences ripple through the entire architecture of your system. In the same way that civil laws regulate access to physical spaces, DCL governs access to the digital sanctuaries where your data resides.

As we leave behind the enforcement mechanisms of DCL, we now turn to the expressive voice of SQL: the SELECT statement. The next chapter introduces Data Query Language (DQL), where the real art of database interaction begins. If DCL is about "who gets to knock on the door," DQL is about "what you say when you open it." Prepare to explore the depth and elegance of querying, aggregation, filtering, grouping, and more. The adventure continues—this time, with questions.

10. SQL Dialects

Introduction

While SQL is standardized by the American National Standards Institute (ANSI), most database systems implement their own dialects—customized versions of SQL that extend or modify the core syntax. These variations can include different data types, built-in functions, procedural extensions, and error handling conventions. Understanding these differences is crucial for developers working across platforms or migrating between systems. In this chapter, we'll explore the major SQL dialects, highlight key distinctions, and provide migration tips and compatibility considerations. Knowing how dialects diverge allows you to write portable, adaptable, and efficient SQL code.

Major SQL Dialects

MySQL

MySQL is one of the most popular and widely adopted open-source relational database management systems (RDBMS), especially favored for web development, startup environments, and applications requiring high-speed read performance. Originally developed by MySQL AB in the mid-1990s, it gained popularity due to its simplicity, fast setup, lightweight footprint, and excellent integration with PHP and other LAMP-stack technologies. After being acquired by Sun Microsystems in 2008 and then by Oracle Corporation in 2010, MySQL has continued to evolve with enhancements in reliability, tooling, and community support. As a core component of millions of dynamic websites and applications—including WordPress, Drupal, and Magento—MySQL plays a foundational role in modern web architecture.

One of the distinguishing characteristics of MySQL is its use of backticks (column) to denote delimited identifiers such as table or column names, which allows the inclusion of reserved words or special characters. This differs from systems like PostgreSQL or Oracle, which use double quotes for this purpose. However, MySQL lacks support for full outer joins out-of-the-box. To simulate a full outer join, developers typically write a UNION of LEFT JOIN and RIGHT JOIN queries while using IS NULL filters. This limitation reflects MySQL's initial prioritization of simplicity and speed over feature completeness.

MySQL employs the LIMIT clause to control the number of rows returned in a query, which is particularly useful for pagination and performance tuning. Combined with OFFSET, developers can retrieve slices of large datasets for use in web interfaces or RESTful APIs. Procedural SQL in MySQL is somewhat restricted compared to more robust implementations like PL/pgSQL (PostgreSQL) or PL/SQL (Oracle). MySQL's block structure begins with BEGIN...END, and its control-of-flow structures include IF, LOOP, and WHILE. However, some features like exception propagation or advanced looping constructs are limited in their flexibility, making complex procedural programming more challenging in MySQL compared to its counterparts.

For error handling, MySQL uses the DECLARE HANDLER syntax, which includes CONTINUE and EXIT handlers that can intercept specific SQLSTATE errors. This can be used to gracefully recover from common conditions like constraint violations or division by zero during procedural execution. However, MySQL does not provide native support for nested exception blocks or user-defined exception hierarchies. This means that while you can catch and handle certain errors, you must often rely on manual error codes and cautious transaction control for more advanced use cases.

MySQL supports multiple storage engines, with InnoDB and MyISAM being the most notable. InnoDB is the default engine for transactional integrity, offering ACID compliance, row-level locking, and support for foreign keys. In contrast, MyISAM is non-transactional, faster for read-heavy workloads, and historically used for full-text search. Each storage engine has trade-offs in performance, durability, and concurrency behavior, and developers must choose based on workload requirements. InnoDB's crash recovery and automatic checkpointing make it well-suited for applications that prioritize data consistency, while MyISAM might be chosen for large-scale read-only reporting environments where performance is critical.

MySQL also includes useful features such as replication, partitioning, and support for spatial data types. Replication supports master-slave and group replication configurations, enabling scaling read workloads or creating high-availability clusters. Partitioning allows large tables to be broken into logical segments to improve query performance, especially in OLAP use cases. Spatial extensions support GIS applications by enabling geographic data storage and spatial indexing. The MySQL Query Optimizer, while relatively simple compared to systems like PostgreSQL, continues to improve with each release and now includes support for hash joins, cost-based analysis, and parallel query evaluation (depending on edition).

Despite its limitations, MySQL remains a cornerstone of relational data solutions due to its speed, ecosystem support, and ease of use. It is supported by powerful tools such as MySQL Workbench, phpMyAdmin, and commercial variants like MariaDB and Percona Server that offer enhanced features and performance. MySQL also integrates easily with cloud-native solutions such as Amazon RDS, Google Cloud SQL, and Azure Database for MySQL, making it a practical choice for both on-premises and cloud-based deployments. For developers and teams that prioritize speed, simplicity, and wide compatibility, MySQL remains a powerful and dependable RDBMS option in the modern data landscape.

PostgreSQL

PostgreSQL is widely celebrated as one of the most powerful, extensible, and standards-compliant open-source relational database systems available today. Originating from the POSTGRES project at the University of California, Berkeley in the mid-1980s, PostgreSQL (originally named POSTGRES95) was conceived as a successor to Ingres, an early pioneering RDBMS. Its design philosophy emphasized support for complex data types, extensibility, and adherence to relational theory—values that continue to define the system decades later.

Often described as the "developer's database," PostgreSQL is renowned for its advanced features, rock-solid reliability, and tight adherence to the SQL standard (including full support for SQL:2011 features). It allows developers to extend the database with custom data types, functions, operators, and even index methods, making it ideal for complex, domain-specific applications in fields such as finance, scientific computing, and geospatial analytics.

From a syntactic standpoint, PostgreSQL uses double quotes ("column") to denote delimited identifiers, preserving case sensitivity and allowing reserved keywords to be used as column or table names. Unlike MySQL, which uses backticks, this aligns with the ANSI SQL standard and improves portability for developers familiar with cross-platform tools.

PostgreSQL's approach to autoincrementing fields is flexible and standards-aware. Traditionally, developers used the SERIAL pseudo-type, which implicitly creates a sequence object and sets the column's default value to pull from it. More recently, PostgreSQL introduced GENERATED ALWAYS AS IDENTITY and GENERATED BY DEFAULT AS IDENTITY, aligning with SQL:2003 standards and giving finer control over identity columns—allowing specification of increment steps, minimum/maximum values, and behavior during INSERT operations.

One of PostgreSQL's most notable features is the RETURNING clause, which enhances Data Manipulation Language (DML) commands like INSERT, UPDATE, and DELETE by returning affected rows without requiring a separate SELECT. This is particularly useful in applications that need to immediately retrieve generated IDs or modified values.

```
INSERT INTO orders
(customer_id, total)
VALUES (42, 150.75)
RETURNING order_id, total;
```

This query both inserts a new order and immediately returns the generated order_id, streamlining workflows and reducing round-trips to the database.

PostgreSQL also supports Common Table Expressions (CTEs) through the WITH clause. CTEs provide a powerful, modular way to write complex queries by breaking them into named subqueries that can be referenced later in the same statement. This improves readability and maintainability of long SQL scripts.

```
WITH recent_orders AS (
SELECT * FROM orders
WHERE order_date >
CURRENT_DATE - INTERVAL '30 days'
)
SELECT customer_id, COUNT(*)
FROM recent_orders
GROUP BY customer_id;
```

This example defines a temporary result set of recent orders and then uses it to count recent purchases by customer.

In terms of procedural logic, PostgreSQL allows for sophisticated scripting through PL/pgSQL, a robust procedural language that supports loops, conditionals, exception handling, and dynamic SQL. For ad hoc or one-off scripts, PostgreSQL also provides anonymous DO blocks, enabling quick execution of logic without the need to define stored procedures.

```
DO $$
BEGIN
IF EXISTS (SELECT 1
FROM users WHERE email
IS NULL) THEN
RAISE NOTICE
'There are users with missing
email addresses.';
END IF;
END;
```

This facilitates powerful control-of-flow constructs embedded directly into SQL workflows. Beyond PL/pgSQL, PostgreSQL supports additional procedural languages such as PL/Perl, PL/Python, and PL/V8 (JavaScript), allowing polyglot programming inside the database engine itself. Another hallmark of PostgreSQL is its commitment to extensibility. Developers can create custom operators, define user-defined types (UDTs), implement custom index access methods (e.g., GIN, GiST, BRIN), and register foreign data wrappers (FDWs) to query external systems like MongoDB, CSV files, or other PostgreSQL servers.

This design enables PostgreSQL to function not just as a relational engine but as a general-purpose data processing framework. PostgreSQL includes robust full-text search capabilities built into the core engine. Using data types like 'tsvector' and 'tsquery', developers can create efficient indexes for natural language search, supporting stemming, tokenization, ranking, and weighting. These features make PostgreSQL an alternative to dedicated search systems for many use cases. Table inheritance, though not commonly used in most RDBMSs, is another advanced feature supported by PostgreSQL.

It allows one table to inherit the structure of another, enabling polymorphic queries and modeling of class hierarchies. While modern usage trends lean more toward JSONB columns and lateral joins for similar purposes, inheritance remains useful in specialized contexts. PostgreSQL is highly ACID-compliant and offers fine-grained control over concurrency with its implementation of Multi-Version Concurrency Control (MVCC).

This means multiple users can read and write data simultaneously without locking conflicts, a critical requirement in high-transactional environments. Developers can also define isolation levels, from 'READ COMMITTED' to 'SERIALIZABLE', giving strong guarantees over data visibility. The PostgreSQL optimizer is advanced and configurable. It uses a cost-based approach to choose optimal query plans, leveraging statistics on column distribution, index selectivity, and join cardinality.

You can influence plan selection using query hints (via configuration settings), analyze execution with 'EXPLAIN ANALYZE', and tune performance with indexes, materialized views, and query rewriting. In terms of deployment and management, PostgreSQL supports powerful replication models—including streaming replication, logical replication, and physical backups. Extensions like 'pglogical', 'Barman', and 'pgBackRest' further enhance backup, restore, and failover capabilities.

PostgreSQL is also well-supported in the cloud via services such as Amazon RDS for PostgreSQL, Google Cloud SQL, Azure Database for PostgreSQL, and specialized platforms like Crunchy Bridge and Neon. Security in PostgreSQL is handled through a combination of roles, schemas, and GRANT-based permissions. Role-based access control (RBAC) is implemented using granular permissions, which can be layered using schemas, database roles, and attribute-level restrictions (such as RLS—Row-Level Security).

Integration with LDAP, PAM, SSL/TLS, and certificate-based authentication enables PostgreSQL to comply with enterprise-grade security requirements. As for the future, PostgreSQL continues to evolve rapidly. The active development community contributes new features each release cycle, including just-in-time (JIT) compilation, parallel queries, JSON manipulation functions, temporal tables, and declarative partitioning.

With native support for semi-structured data ('JSONB'), PostgreSQL increasingly bridges the gap between traditional relational models and NoSQL flexibility, making it an appealing choice for hybrid applications. In summary, PostgreSQL is not just a relational database; it is a data platform. From its academic origins to its modern enterprise-grade capabilities, PostgreSQL blends the best of traditional SQL, extensibility, and performance.

Whether you're building real-time analytics systems, powering a web application, or designing a complex ETL pipeline, PostgreSQL offers the depth, transparency, and control to get the job done right. — Let me know if you'd like visuals or comparative tables with MySQL, Oracle, or SQL Server.

SQL Server (T-SQL)

Microsoft SQL Server uses a variant of SQL known as **T-SQL** (Transact-SQL), which extends the ANSI SQL standard with powerful procedural programming capabilities, error handling constructs, and system-level tools. It is widely used in enterprise environments, especially in Microsoft-centered ecosystems, for applications ranging from web services and business intelligence to mission-critical transactional systems.

Delimited Identifiers and Syntax

Unlike most RDBMSs that use double quotes or backticks, SQL Server uses **square brackets** [ ] to enclose identifiers that contain spaces, reserved keywords, or special characters:

```
SELECT [First Name],
[Order Date]
FROM [Sales Orders];
```

You can also use double quotes by setting QUOTED_IDENTIFIER ON, but square brackets remain the standard.

Procedural Logic: BEGIN...END

T-SQL supports control-of-flow language constructs such as:

- BEGIN...END blocks for grouping statements
- IF...ELSE for conditional logic
- WHILE loops
- GOTO for manual flow control
- RETURN statements in stored procedures or functions

Example:

```
IF EXISTS (SELECT * FROM users WHERE id = 1)
BEGIN
UPDATE users SET status = 'active' WHERE id = 1;
END
ELSE
BEGIN
PRINT 'User not found.';
END
```

Error Handling with TRY...CATCH

T-SQL provides structured error handling through TRY...CATCH blocks. This enables robust database programming by allowing developers to catch and respond to runtime errors:

```
BEGIN TRY
INSERT INTO accounts
(id, balance)
VALUES (1, 1000);
END TRY
BEGIN CATCH
PRINT 'An error occurred: '
+ ERROR_MESSAGE();
END CATCH
```

Within a CATCH block, functions like ERROR_MESSAGE(), ERROR_NUMBER(), and ERROR_LINE() provide detailed diagnostics.

Limiting Results: TOP N and OFFSET...FETCH

Instead of the ANSI-standard LIMIT clause, SQL Server uses the TOP keyword:

```
SELECT TOP 5 *
FROM products
ORDER BY price DESC;
```

With SQL Server 2012 and later, you can also use the ANSI-compliant OFFSET...FETCH clause:

```
SELECT * FROM products
ORDER BY price DESC
OFFSET 0 ROWS FETCH NEXT 5 ROWS ONLY;
```

Built-in Functions

SQL Server includes numerous proprietary functions, including:

- GETDATE() — returns the current system timestamp
- NEWID() — generates a new GUID
- ISNULL() and COALESCE() — handle NULL values
- CONVERT() and CAST() — perform data type conversions
- CHARINDEX(), PATINDEX() — search within strings
- DATEADD(), DATEDIFF(), EOMONTH() — perform date arithmetic

Example:

```
SELECT GETDATE() AS current_time;
```

Transactions and Isolation Levels

SQL Server provides full **ACID-compliant** transactional support, with advanced control over **isolation levels** and **locking behavior**.

Supported isolation levels:

- READ UNCOMMITTED (dirty reads allowed)
- READ COMMITTED (default)
- REPEATABLE READ
- SNAPSHOT (uses row versioning)
- SERIALIZABLE (most strict)

Example:

```
SET TRANSACTION ISOLATION LEVEL SERIALIZABLE;
BEGIN TRANSACTION;
—operations
COMMIT;
```

SQL Server also supports the WITH (NOLOCK) hint to override isolation level on a per-query basis, though it should be used with caution due to potential data anomalies.

Triggers and Procedural Automation

T-SQL supports three types of triggers:

- **AFTER triggers** — execute after DML operations (INSERT, UPDATE, DELETE)
- **INSTEAD OF triggers** — override standard DML behavior
- **DDL triggers** — respond to schema-level events (CREATE, ALTER, DROP)

Example:

```
CREATE TRIGGER trg_after_insert
ON orders
AFTER INSERT
AS
BEGIN
PRINT 'A new order has been inserted.';
END;
```

Views, Functions, and Stored Procedures

T-SQL makes extensive use of modular components:

- **Views** — reusable SELECT statements
- **Scalar and table-valued functions** — encapsulate reusable logic
- **Stored Procedures** — manage multi-step operations with input/output parameters

Example stored procedure:

```
CREATE PROCEDURE sp_get_user_orders
@UserId INT
AS
BEGIN
SELECT * FROM orders WHERE user_id = @UserId;
END;
```

These objects promote code reuse, enhance performance, and improve abstraction.

Integration Features

T-SQL is also deeply integrated into the Microsoft ecosystem:

- **SQL Server Agent** — for job scheduling and automation
- **SQL Server Reporting Services (SSRS)** — for dashboarding and reporting
- **SQL Server Integration Services (SSIS)** — for ETL pipelines and data warehousing
- **Azure SQL** — for managed cloud-based deployment

It also supports integration with CLR (Common Language Runtime), enabling stored procedures to be written in .NET languages such as C# or VB.NET.

Summary

T-SQL's strengths include:

- Rich procedural logic and error handling
- Fine-grained transaction control
- Deep integration with Microsoft data services
- Robust tools for automation, reporting, and cloud deployment

Its distinctive syntax (e.g., TOP, square brackets, TRY...CATCH) and function library give SQL Server a unique identity in the SQL ecosystem. SQL Server is an excellent choice for data-heavy enterprise systems that require scalability, reliability, and integration with Microsoft's stack.

Oracle (PL/SQL)

Oracle's PL/SQL (Procedural Language/Structured Query Language) is one of the most powerful SQL extensions available in any RDBMS. It combines SQL's declarative power with procedural constructs like loops, conditionals, exceptions, and modular programming elements (such as procedures, functions, packages, and triggers). This hybrid capability makes Oracle a leading choice for large-scale enterprise applications, financial institutions, and government systems where business logic is often embedded within the database layer itself.

PL/SQL starts with a DECLARE block to define variables, cursors, and types, followed by a BEGIN block for logic and optionally an EXCEPTION block for error handling. Here's a minimal PL/SQL program structure:

```
DECLARE
v_total_sales NUMBER;
BEGIN
SELECT SUM(amount)
INTO v_total_sales
FROM sales
WHERE sale_date
>= SYSDATE - 30;
DBMS_OUTPUT.PUT_LINE
('Total sales: ' || v_total_sales);
EXCEPTION
WHEN OTHERS THEN
DBMS_OUTPUT.PUT_LINE
('An error occurred.');
END;
```

PL/SQL allows you to create:

- **Procedures and Functions** for reusable blocks of logic
- **Packages** that group related procedures/functions together
- **Cursors** for row-by-row processing
- **Triggers** that automatically execute on specific table events
- **User-defined Exceptions** for custom error control

Oracle uses double quotes ("ColumnName") to reference case-sensitive or reserved identifiers. For row-limiting, earlier versions relied on ROWNUM, but modern versions support ANSI-standard FETCH FIRST N ROWS ONLY syntax:

```
SELECT * FROM employees
FETCH FIRST 5 ROWS ONLY;
```

Instead of using AUTO_INCREMENT or SERIAL, Oracle relies on SEQUENCE objects and optionally TRIGGERS to generate unique values for primary keys:

```
CREATE SEQUENCE emp_seq
```

```
START WITH 1 INCREMENT BY 1;
CREATE TABLE employees (
id NUMBER PRIMARY KEY,
name VARCHAR2(100)
);
CREATE OR REPLACE
TRIGGER emp_trigger
BEFORE INSERT ON employees
FOR EACH ROW
BEGIN
SELECT emp_seq.NEXTVAL
INTO :NEW.id FROM dual;
END;
```

These advanced features make Oracle a high-end, programmable platform ideal for logic-heavy applications—but with complexity comes a learning curve and licensing cost.

SQLite

SQLite is a self-contained, serverless, zero-configuration SQL engine embedded directly into applications. It's widely adopted in mobile apps (e.g., Android and iOS), IoT devices, web browsers, and desktop software for local storage due to its simplicity, portability, and reliability.

Despite being compact, SQLite supports most of the SQL-92 standard and includes many advanced features:

- Transactions (with full ACID compliance)
- Triggers
- Views
- Virtual tables via FTS5 (Full-Text Search)
- JSON support via json_functions

However, SQLite takes a different approach to typing: it uses **dynamic typing**, where a column declared as INTEGER may still accept text or blobs unless explicitly constrained. This flexibility is convenient for prototyping but can lead to inconsistencies if not carefully managed.

Example:

```
CREATE TABLE notes (
id INTEGER
```

```
PRIMARY KEY,
content TEXT NOT NULL,
created_at DATETIME
DEFAULT CURRENT_TIMESTAMP
);
```

SQLite supports row limits via the familiar LIMIT clause:

```
SELECT * FROM notes LIMIT 10;
```

What SQLite lacks:

- No built-in RIGHT JOIN or FULL OUTER JOIN
- Limited concurrency (supports only one writer at a time)
- No native stored procedures or packages
- Weaker enforcement of strict schema constraints unless using strict tables (STRICT keyword added in version 3.37.0)

SQLite's design makes it ideal for scenarios like:

- Mobile app data storage (e.g., WhatsApp chat history)
- Desktop app settings or caches
- Client-side data storage in web browsers
- Rapid prototyping or testing without needing a database server

It supports single-file databases, is open source (public domain), and is renowned for being highly stable. Still, it is not recommended for high-concurrency environments or enterprise-scale transactional workloads.

Comparison Table

Feature	MySQL	Postgre SQL	SQL Server	Oracle
Delimited Identifiers	‘column‘	"column"	[column]	"column"
Result Limiting	LIMIT	LIMIT / FETCH	TOP N	ROWNUM / FETCH
Procedural Extension	BEGIN... END	DO blocks	BEGIN... END, TRY... CATCH	DECLARE ... BEGIN ... END
Auto increment Field	AUTO_ INCREMENT	SERIAL, GENE -RATED	IDENTITY	SEQUENCE + TRIGGER
Error Handling	DECLARE HANDLER	EXCEP -TION	TRY... CATCH	EXCEP -TION

Portability Tips

- Always use ANSI-standard syntax when possible.
- Avoid proprietary functions unless absolutely necessary.
- Use views and stored procedures to encapsulate dialect-specific logic.
- Rely on migration tools and ORMs that abstract over dialect differences.
- Regularly test your SQL on the target DBMS to catch incompatibilities early.

Conclusion

Though SQL dialects share a common foundation, the practical differences among them can affect how you write, optimize, and maintain code. By learning the strengths and quirks of each dialect, you'll gain the flexibility to build applications across diverse platforms. Whether you're querying PostgreSQL on the backend or using MySQL in a WordPress site, the concepts you've mastered in standard SQL will remain relevant. SQL's adaptability across dialects is a testament to its enduring power as a language. Embrace the dialects not as limitations, but as pathways to deeper fluency and strategic development.

11. Advanced SQL

Introduction

As your SQL expertise grows, so does the breadth and complexity of tasks you'll be expected to master. This chapter plunges into the most sophisticated and powerful aspects of SQL, unlocking new layers of data processing capabilities. Advanced SQL enables intricate data modeling, performance tuning, and multi-step logic encapsulation that are vital for analytics, reporting, machine learning pipelines, and enterprise-grade applications. With topics ranging from Common Table Expressions and recursion to JSON manipulation and procedural logic, this chapter equips you with an essential toolkit. Proficiency here doesn't just improve productivity—it elevates your SQL fluency to a professional standard capable of solving real-world data challenges.

Beyond the basic data retrieval and modification tasks that most SQL users start with, advanced SQL introduces structural thinking and problem decomposition. Rather than solving problems row by row, it encourages you to think in terms of sets, windows, sequences, hierarchies, and temporal patterns. It enables you to build dynamic solutions that are robust, scalable, and maintainable.

Advanced SQL techniques often blend declarative syntax with procedural constructs. For example, recursive Common Table Expressions (CTEs) allow you to walk hierarchies such as organization charts or file directories; window functions let you evaluate trends, rankings, and comparisons without collapsing data; stored procedures automate multi-step logic on the database server itself. Other tools like materialized views and indexed expressions optimize complex calculations.

Whether you are performing ETL (Extract, Transform, Load), developing dynamic reporting dashboards, or tuning long-running queries on big data systems, these techniques unlock performance and sophistication. You'll also learn to reduce redundancy and improve maintainability through modular patterns like reusable subqueries and views. You'll discover the power of metadata queries and dynamic SQL for introspective systems.

Mastering advanced SQL transforms your role: from script-writer to architect, from data consumer to data engineer. You gain the ability to think algorithmically within the constraints and optimizations of relational algebra. This chapter is your gateway to becoming fluent in the language of data.

Historical Background of Advanced SQL Techniques

The need for advanced SQL techniques emerged as relational databases matured and data volumes exploded. SQL began in the 1970s at IBM with the System R project, where Donald D. Chamberlin and Raymond F. Boyce introduced SEQUEL (Structured English Query Language). Early SQL handled simple queries, projections, and joins. However, real-world problems quickly demanded more.

In the 1980s and 1990s, enterprise applications needed to model hierarchies, compute aggregates across partitions, and express recursive relationships. This led to the standardization of recursive CTEs and window functions in SQL:1999 and SQL:2003 respectively. These features allowed SQL to move beyond static joins and aggregations into temporal, ordered, and hierarchical domains.

The rise of Business Intelligence (BI) tools, data warehouses, and OLAP systems further expanded SQL's role. As companies built multi-terabyte systems with intricate reporting requirements, SQL had to accommodate summarizations, multi-level filtering, and dynamic pivots. This gave rise to constructs like ROLLUP, CUBE, and GROUPING SETS, making multidimensional analysis possible directly in SQL.

Procedural extensions like PL/SQL (Oracle), T-SQL (SQL Server), and PL/pgSQL (PostgreSQL) allowed developers to embed control flow logic, variable declarations, and error handling directly within SQL environments. These empowered the creation of reusable code objects (procedures, functions, triggers), bringing SQL closer to general-purpose programming languages.

With the explosion of web applications and real-time analytics, JSON and XML support became critical. SQL standards and vendors adapted by introducing native JSON data types, path expressions, and manipulation functions. PostgreSQL led the way with advanced JSONB indexing and functions, soon followed by MySQL and SQL Server.

The evolution of SQL dialects was driven not only by user demands but also by technological shifts: from mainframes to distributed systems, from batch jobs to interactive queries, and from rigid schemas to semi-structured formats. The tools of advanced SQL are a response to these evolutionary pressures, enabling developers to meet new performance, scalability, and flexibility requirements while staying within the relational model.

Today, advanced SQL is indispensable. Whether you're cleaning massive datasets, defining data lakes, or powering ML feature stores, it is the bridge between raw data and strategic action. Understanding where these techniques came from helps us appreciate their design intent and apply them with purpose.

1. Common Table Expressions (CTEs)

Common Table Expressions (CTEs) are a game-changing abstraction for writing modular SQL. They define named temporary result sets used within a larger query, improving both readability and reusability. CTEs are particularly helpful when decomposing nested queries, encapsulating business logic, or simplifying joins across multiple steps.

```
WITH recent_books AS (
SELECT * FROM books
WHERE published_year > 2020
)
SELECT title
FROM recent_books
WHERE author = 'Ngugi';
```

You can chain multiple CTEs and even reference them in subsequent CTEs. Many database engines also optimize CTEs internally, improving performance for repeated calculations. CTEs are invaluable for breaking down long SQL scripts into testable and readable components.

2. Recursive CTEs

Recursive CTEs are powerful tools for querying hierarchical, nested, or graph-structured data. They function by defining a base case and a recursive part, which repeatedly joins back to the result set until a stopping condition is met.

```
WITH RECURSIVE department_path
(id, name, path) AS (
SELECT id, name, name
FROM departments
WHERE parent_id IS NULL
UNION ALL
SELECT d.id, d.name,
CONCAT(p.path, ' > ', d.name)
FROM departments d
INNER JOIN department_path p
ON p.id = d.parent_id
)
SELECT * FROM department_path;
```

Use cases include parsing org charts, navigating category trees, or finding ancestral and descendant relationships in family data or graph traversal algorithms. Recursive CTEs are a staple of sophisticated SQL logic.

3. Window Functions

Window functions operate across a "window" of rows related to the current row without collapsing results into groups. This allows detailed comparative calculations and rankings while retaining full row visibility.

```
SELECT name, department, salary,
RANK() OVER
(PARTITION BY department
ORDER BY salary DESC)
AS dept_rank
FROM employees;
```

Use cases include running totals, moving averages, cumulative distributions, and time-based analytics. Other examples include ROW_NUMBER(), NTILE(), FIRST_VALUE(), LAST_VALUE(), LAG(), and LEAD(). These tools enable extremely expressive data insights with minimal code.

4. Advanced Aggregation

For multidimensional reporting, advanced aggregation mechanisms like GROUPING SETS, ROLLUP, and CUBE allow aggregate functions to work on different levels of grouping in a single query:

```
SELECT department, role,
COUNT(*)
FROM employees
GROUP BY CUBE
(department, role);
```

This is invaluable for OLAP-style reporting, enabling subtotals, grand totals, and drill-down summaries without requiring multiple separate queries. These commands are powerful when constructing dashboards or pivot-like reports.

5. JSON and XML Handling

Relational databases increasingly support semi-structured data formats like JSON and XML. This hybrid flexibility is essential for modern applications integrating APIs or NoSQL-like structures:

```
SELECT data->>'name'
AS product_name
FROM products WHERE data->>'category'
= 'Books';
```

You can parse, index, search, and even join against JSON and XML fields. In PostgreSQL, use #> and ->> operators; in SQL Server, use JSON_VALUE() or OPENJSON. This blurs the line between relational and document-oriented systems, enhancing schema flexibility.

6. Query Optimization

Advanced SQL isn't just about querying power—it's about efficiency. Using EXPLAIN, EXPLAIN ANALYZE, or graphical execution plans lets you understand exactly how the database interprets your query:

```
EXPLAIN SELECT *
FROM books
WHERE published_year = 2022;
```

Optimization strategies include:

- Creating and indexing relevant columns
- Avoiding wildcard selects (SELECT *)
- Eliminating unnecessary joins or subqueries
- Rewriting complex WHERE clauses
- Using CTEs instead of derived tables where supported

Tuning queries improves responsiveness and minimizes I/O costs—critical for high-traffic databases.

7. Stored Procedures and Triggers

Stored procedures encapsulate multi-step database logic that can be reused and parameterized. They reduce application-side complexity and centralize critical workflows:

```
DELIMITER //
CREATE PROCEDURE RaiseSalary
(IN emp_id INT,
IN percent DECIMAL(5,2))
BEGIN
UPDATE employees
SET salary = salary
* (1 + percent / 100)
WHERE id = emp_id;
END //
DELIMITER ;
```

Triggers allow the database to automatically respond to events like inserts, updates, or deletions:

```
CREATE TRIGGER audit_salary_update
BEFORE UPDATE ON employees
FOR EACH ROW
SET NEW.last_modified = NOW();
```

Use them judiciously for data integrity, audits, or replication mechanisms. Triggers and procedures are the foundation of logic-driven data automation inside the database engine itself.

Conclusion

Advanced SQL capabilities unlock your database's full potential. Whether you're writing recursive reports, optimizing for speed, or integrating semi-structured data, these techniques equip you to solve complex problems elegantly. SQL is not just a query language—it's an expressive framework for logic, analysis, and automation. By mastering these techniques, you empower yourself to become a data expert capable of handling enterprise-level tasks. The next frontier lies in applying SQL to real-world performance and architectural scenarios, where theory meets execution.

End-of-Chapter Humor

- What do you call a subquery that talks too much? A nested overthinker.
- I asked SQL for a sandwich. It gave me a NULL. Must've missed the WHERE clause.
- Why did the window function apply for a promotion? It wanted to move up the rank!
- Don't trust atoms... or cross joins. They both make everything explode.
- SQL's pickup line? "Can I join you on this table?"

12. Beyond SQL

Introduction

While SQL remains dominant in structured data processing, modern applications often demand greater flexibility, scalability, and performance for unstructured or semi-structured data. This has led to the rise of alternative data storage and query paradigms—collectively known as NoSQL. In this chapter, we explore what lies beyond traditional SQL: document stores, key-value databases, graph systems, and semi-structured formats like JSON. These technologies aren't competitors to SQL—they're companions in a growing data landscape.

NoSQL emerged from the limitations of traditional RDBMSs in addressing scalability, performance bottlenecks, and heterogeneous data formats. The growing need for distributed computing, real-time analytics, mobile-first applications, and web-scale architectures has accelerated its adoption. From flexible document models to lightning-fast key-value systems, NoSQL offers developers the tools to tackle diverse challenges in the era of big data, microservices, and global applications.

Historical Evolution of NoSQL and JSON

The rise of NoSQL and JSON technologies is closely tied to the changing landscape of application development, the explosive growth of unstructured data, and the evolution of web-based architectures. Their development represents a paradigm shift from rigid, schema-based relational models toward more flexible, scalable, and developer-friendly approaches.

The Origins of NoSQL

The term "NoSQL" was first coined by Carlo Strozzi in 1998 to describe a lightweight, open-source relational database that did not expose a standard SQL interface. However, the modern use of the term gained traction in 2009, when Johan Oskarsson of Last.fm organized a meetup to discuss distributed, non-relational databases that could handle large-scale data across multiple nodes. The hashtag #NoSQL quickly became a rallying point for a community seeking alternatives to traditional RDBMS solutions like Oracle, SQL Server, and MySQL.

Early NoSQL databases included:

- **Google Bigtable** (2006) – A distributed storage system for managing structured data, built for scalability.
- **Amazon Dynamo** (2007) – A highly available key-value store built to power services like the shopping cart on Amazon.com.
- **Apache Cassandra** (2008) – A hybrid column-store developed at Facebook, influenced by Bigtable and Dynamo.
- **MongoDB** (2009) – A document-oriented database designed to store JSON-like documents, providing flexibility and high performance.

The core motivation behind NoSQL was to solve limitations that relational databases faced in distributed and high-velocity environments:

- **Scalability:** Relational databases scale vertically (by upgrading hardware), while NoSQL databases are designed for horizontal scaling (adding more servers).
- **Schema flexibility:** Traditional RDBMSs require a strict schema, whereas NoSQL systems allow for dynamic or schema-less data models.
- **High availability:** With built-in replication and fault tolerance, NoSQL databases are resilient to node failures.
- **Agility:** Developers can rapidly evolve applications without having to re-engineer schemas.

The Rise of JSON

JSON (JavaScript Object Notation) was developed by Douglas Crockford in the early 2000s as a lightweight data-interchange format. Originally intended for client-server communication in web applications, JSON quickly gained popularity due to its simplicity, human readability, and ease of parsing across most modern programming languages.

Key milestones in JSON's rise include:

- **2001:** Crockford formalized JSON as a text format derived from JavaScript object syntax.
- **2005:** JSON overtook XML in popularity for data transfer on the web, aided by AJAX and RESTful APIs.
- **2013:** JSON became an official IETF standard (RFC 7159), cementing its role in web and mobile ecosystems.

As developers increasingly stored and retrieved data in JSON format, databases evolved to support native JSON operations. PostgreSQL introduced powerful JSON functions and the jsonb datatype; MySQL added JSON support in version 5.7. MongoDB was built from the ground up to treat JSON-like documents as first-class data structures (stored internally as BSON).

Modern Trends and the Blurring Lines

In recent years, the boundary between SQL and NoSQL has become increasingly blurred. Relational databases now support JSON, while some NoSQL systems offer SQL-like querying capabilities. For example:

- **PostgreSQL** supports indexing and querying within JSONB documents.
- **MySQL** allows JSON fields and path-based extraction.
- **Couchbase** provides N1QL, a SQL-like language for querying JSON documents.
- **Google BigQuery** offers semi-structured data support and SQL analytics.

Moreover, the growth of microservices, serverless architecture, and edge computing has created new demands for hybrid solutions that combine the consistency of SQL with the flexibility of NoSQL.

Conclusion

The development of NoSQL and JSON was driven by the needs of modern applications to handle large-scale, rapidly changing, and heterogeneous data. From their roots in solving performance and flexibility bottlenecks, they have grown into mature ecosystems that now complement and extend the relational model. Their evolution reflects the dynamic nature of data management in the cloud era—flexible, scalable, and built for speed.

Types of NoSQL Databases

- **Document Databases:** Store data as JSON-like documents (e.g., MongoDB, CouchDB). Each document is flexible and self-describing, ideal for hierarchical and nested data structures. Collections replace tables, and fields can vary across documents.
- **Key-Value Stores:** Simple, ultra-fast lookup based on unique keys (e.g., Redis, DynamoDB). These are used in caching, session management, and quick retrieval of sparse datasets.
- **Column-Family Stores:** Store data in columns instead of rows for high performance on distributed systems (e.g., Apache Cassandra, HBase). Suited for analytical queries, time-series data, and write-heavy workloads.
- **Graph Databases:** Focus on relationships between data points, ideal for social networks, fraud detection, or recommendation systems (e.g., Neo4j, Amazon Neptune). Nodes and edges are first-class citizens.
- **Time-Series Databases:** Specialized for timestamped data, such as metrics and logs (e.g., InfluxDB, TimescaleDB). Designed to efficiently store, compress, and query temporal data.
- **Multi-Model Databases:** Support multiple data paradigms in one engine (e.g., ArangoDB, OrientDB).

Why NoSQL?

- **Scalability:** NoSQL databases often scale horizontally, making them suitable for big data and cloud-native environments. Partitioning and sharding are first-class capabilities.
- **Flexibility:** No rigid schema needed. Each record can have a different structure. This suits agile development and data evolution.
- **Speed:** Optimized for specific data access patterns—real-time analytics, key-value lookups, or graph traversals. Writes and reads can be significantly faster in the absence of schema validation and joins.
- **Agility:** Developers can iterate faster without constant schema migrations. Rapid prototyping and release cycles are easier to manage.
- **Fault Tolerance:** Designed with high availability and replication in mind. Some NoSQL systems can survive node failures without downtime.
- **High Write Throughput:** Ideal for IoT, telemetry, and streaming use cases.

JSON and Semi-Structured Data

JavaScript Object Notation (JSON) has become a de facto standard for transmitting and storing semi-structured data, not just in web APIs but increasingly within enterprise-grade databases. JSON provides a flexible, human-readable, and language-agnostic format to represent complex, nested structures such as arrays, objects, and key-value mappings. As applications began to evolve beyond rigid table schemas, developers demanded the ability to store heterogeneous and hierarchical data more naturally—and JSON filled that need.

Modern relational databases now support native JSON fields (e.g., MySQL's `JSON` type, PostgreSQL's `jsonb`, SQL Server's JSON functions), enabling powerful hybrid queries that operate on both structured and semi-structured data. These JSON fields can be indexed, queried, updated, and validated with increasing sophistication, allowing SQL to function as a semi-document-oriented query engine.

This hybrid capability bridges the best of both worlds—SQL's strong consistency and relational logic with NoSQL's flexibility and schema-on-read model. JSON data can be queried using arrow operators (e.g., -> or ->>), JSON path expressions, or even full-text search extensions in some systems. This integration makes it easier to ingest logs, user settings, preferences, sensor data, or metadata directly into a SQL-based pipeline without normalization bottlenecks.

Advanced Example: Storing and Querying JSON in PostgreSQL

```
CREATE TABLE products (
    id SERIAL PRIMARY KEY,
    name TEXT,
    attributes JSONB,
    created_at TIMESTAMP DEFAULT NOW()
    );
    INSERT INTO products (name, attributes)
    VALUES
    ('T-Shirt', '{"size": "M",
    "color": "blue", "stock": 35}'),
    ('Jeans', '{"size": "L",
    "color": "black", "stock": 10}'),
    ('Shoes', '{"size": 9,
    "color": "white", "stock": 0,
    "tags": ["clearance", "summer"]}');
    —Query products with
    specific attribute values
    SELECT name, attributes->>'color'
    AS color
    FROM products
    WHERE attributes->>'stock'::int > '0';
    —Indexing JSON keys for performance
    CREATE INDEX
    idx_products_attributes_stock
    ON products
    ((attributes->>'stock'));
    —Updating a JSON field
    UPDATE products
    SET attributes
    = jsonb_set
```

```
(attributes, '{stock}',
'"50"', false)
WHERE name = 'Shoes';
```

This example demonstrates PostgreSQL's ability to handle JSON queries, updates, and indexing, showcasing the versatility and performance potential of semi-structured data handling within SQL.

When to Use NoSQL Over SQL

While SQL systems have evolved to accommodate many use cases involving semi-structured data, NoSQL databases still offer advantages under specific conditions. Choosing NoSQL over SQL should be a deliberate decision based on the nature of the workload, scalability requirements, and development priorities.

- **Schema is highly dynamic or unknown:** Projects with rapidly evolving data structures—such as prototypes, MVPs, or microservices—benefit from schema-less databases like MongoDB or Couchbase.
- **Massive-scale workloads:** Applications needing petabyte-scale data spread across hundreds of servers (e.g., IoT platforms, analytics backends) are often better served by horizontally scalable NoSQL systems.
- **Extremely high write/read throughput:** Use NoSQL when working with streaming ingestion, sensor networks, or clickstream analytics where latency and performance are more critical than normalization.
- **Graph-based relationships:** When relationships between data points (like friends, follows, or paths) are central to the application logic, graph databases like Neo4j or Amazon Neptune offer intuitive querying and better performance than SQL joins.
- **Irregular, polymorphic data:** NoSQL shines in storing user-generated content, preferences, or configuration objects that may vary widely between records.
- **Offline-first or disconnected systems:** NoSQL systems with embedded support (e.g., PouchDB, Realm) are ideal for mobile or

edge computing environments.

- **Frequent schema evolution:** Teams that iterate quickly without formal DBAs often prefer NoSQL for the reduced overhead in altering data structures.
- **Event sourcing and log retention:** Key-value and columnar stores are often preferred for high-ingest, write-once-read-many workloads such as audit trails or time-series event data.

Ultimately, NoSQL and SQL are not adversaries. Many mature systems employ both: using SQL for structured financial data and transactions, and NoSQL for caching, personalization, or metadata. Choosing the right tool ensures long-term scalability, developer agility, and system resilience.

Hybrid Approaches

Many modern systems combine SQL and NoSQL technologies for the best of both worlds:

- Use SQL databases for financial transactions, and document stores for user-generated content or logs.
- Store clickstream data in time-series databases like InfluxDB while using relational systems for reporting.
- Use NoSQL to buffer real-time ingestion and later transfer summaries into SQL for business intelligence.
- Leverage cloud-native solutions like Google BigQuery, Amazon Aurora, or Azure Cosmos DB, which support polyglot persistence and allow SQL queries on document or graph data.

In summary, SQL and NoSQL technologies are not in opposition. Choosing the right one depends on your use case, workload pattern, and team expertise. As database ecosystems evolve, learning to speak both SQL and NoSQL fluently will be essential for developers and data professionals alike.

Conclusion

SQL taught us to think in terms of structure, precision, and integrity. NoSQL teaches us to think in terms of flexibility, scalability, and speed. Together, they give us the best of both worlds. Mastering SQL doesn't mean ignoring NoSQL—it means knowing when to use the right tool for the job. As your projects grow in complexity, understanding modern data models will allow you to build systems that scale smartly and adapt quickly.

End-of-Chapter Humor

- Why did the SQL developer break up with the NoSQL database? It kept things too casual.
- SQL says: "I require commitment and structure." NoSQL replies: "I'm more of a free spirit."
- MongoDB tried to date a relational database once—it found the relationship too restrictive.
- PostgreSQL to JSON: "You're not my type." JSON: "But I can be anything you want!"

13. Practical Projects

Introduction

SQL is best understood not just by reading syntax but by building real-world applications. This chapter walks you through practical, hands-on projects that synthesize everything you've learned. These projects range in complexity from basic database design to more advanced reporting and data integration tasks. Each one highlights different SQL sublanguages and techniques, helping you gain confidence through application. Whether you're pursuing a career in development, analytics, or administration, these exercises will sharpen your SQL thinking.

Bookstore Inventory System

Overview

Design a database for a bookstore that handles book inventory, authors, genres, and customer orders.

Schema Requirements

- books table — stores ID, title, author_id, genre_id, price, stock quantity.
- authors table — stores author ID and name.
- genres table — stores genre ID and name.
- customers table — stores customer ID, name, and contact info.
- orders table — stores order ID, customer ID, date.
- order_items table — stores order ID, book ID, quantity.

Key Learning Objectives

- Use of DDL to define tables and keys.
- Use of DML to populate and update records.
- Writing JOINs to track order histories and inventory levels.

- Implementing transactions (TCL) to ensure orders and stock updates are atomic.

Employee Timesheet System

Overview

Create a time tracking system for employees and departments across a medium-sized company.

Schema Requirements

- employees — ID, name, department_id, hire_date.
- departments — ID, name.
- timesheets — timesheet ID, employee ID, date, hours worked, project name.

Key Learning Objectives

- Creating relationships using foreign keys.
- Querying total hours worked per employee, per project.
- Using aggregate functions like SUM, AVG, and GROUP BY.
- Practice with subqueries to find anomalies (e.g., overtime).

Movie Recommendation System

Overview

Design the foundation for a movie streaming service's recommendation engine.

Schema Requirements

- users — user ID, username, join date.
- movies — movie ID, title, genre ID, release year.
- genres — genre ID, name.
- ratings — user ID, movie ID, rating, timestamp.

Key Learning Objectives

- Querying top-rated movies by genre and time.
- Creating views and indexes for performance optimization.
- Using window functions to calculate running averages.
- Designing a schema that scales to large userbases.

Normalization in a CRM System

Scenario

An organization initially stored all customer interaction data in one table, resulting in redundancy and inconsistency. Your task is to normalize the design.

Steps

- Identify repeating groups (e.g., multiple contacts in a single cell).
- Break into separate tables for contacts, interaction logs, accounts.
- Define primary and foreign keys.
- Write queries that demonstrate how normalization improves data accuracy.

Data Corruption Recovery

Scenario

A script erroneously deleted records from the payments table in a financial system. You have to recover using SQL backups and transaction logs.

Steps

- Use ROLLBACK or point-in-time recovery features (if available).
- Query backups or shadow tables for recent changes.
- Analyze with JOINs and aggregate functions to identify missing patterns.
- Set up safeguards like BEFORE DELETE triggers going forward.

E-Commerce Shopping Cart System

Overview

Build a simplified schema to track user shopping carts and checkouts for an e-commerce platform.

Schema Requirements

- users — user ID, name, email.
- products — product ID, name, price, stock.
- cart — cart ID, user ID, creation timestamp.
- cart_items — cart ID, product ID, quantity.

Key Learning Objectives

- Tracking temporary vs. committed purchases.
- Using JOINs to build cart summaries.
- Demonstrating data validation on stock levels.
- Applying transaction logic during checkout.

Hospital Patient Management System

Overview

Develop a system to track patient visits, doctors, and diagnoses in a clinical setting.

Schema Requirements

- patients — patient ID, name, DOB.
- doctors — doctor ID, name, specialty.
- visits — visit ID, patient ID, doctor ID, date.
- diagnoses — diagnosis ID, visit ID, description.

Key Learning Objectives

- Representing one-to-many relationships.
- Auditing medical history through JOINs.
- Querying for doctor caseloads.
- Designing for confidentiality and role-based access.

Library Book Lending System

Overview

Construct a schema to manage book loans in a library setting.

Schema Requirements

- books — book ID, title, author, status.
- members — member ID, name, join date.
- loans — loan ID, book ID, member ID, issue date, due date.

Key Learning Objectives

- Creating constraints to avoid double-loaning.
- Tracking overdue books using date functions.
- Implementing views for active loans.
- Writing triggers for automatic due date notifications.

Food Delivery Platform

Overview

Model a food delivery system connecting restaurants, couriers, and customers.

Schema Requirements

- restaurants — restaurant ID, name, location.
- menu_items — item ID, restaurant ID, name, price.

- customers — customer ID, name, address.
- orders — order ID, customer ID, restaurant ID, courier ID, timestamp.
- order_details — order ID, item ID, quantity.
- couriers — courier ID, name, vehicle.

Key Learning Objectives

- Designing many-to-many relationships.
- Querying average delivery times and top restaurants.
- Using aggregation to rank couriers.
- Applying filters and subqueries for restaurant analytics.

Online Education Platform

Overview

Develop the schema for a course enrollment and tracking system.

Schema Requirements

- students — student ID, name, email.
- courses — course ID, title, instructor.
- enrollments — student ID, course ID, enrollment date.
- progress — student ID, course ID, lesson, completion status.

Key Learning Objectives

- Working with composite primary keys.
- Joining across multiple levels of detail.
- Writing queries to show student progress.
- Designing for scalability across thousands of students.

Project Tips and Best Practices

- **Start small.** Don't try to model the entire system at once—build core functionality first.

- **Normalize gradually.** Over-normalization can lead to performance issues.
- **Write test data.** Always populate test rows before building queries.
- **Back up often.** Especially before running DELETE, UPDATE, or structural changes.
- **Comment your queries.** Leave notes in complex SQL for yourself and teammates.

Conclusion

These projects are designed to give you a real sense of SQL's utility in the wild. They also teach you to think relationally—mapping business processes to tables, fields, and keys. Whether you're modeling an e-commerce store or handling high-volume analytics, these exercises sharpen both your technical skill and your database intuition. The more you build, the more you'll internalize the logic of SQL. Don't stop at these examples—start inventing your own.

End-of-Chapter Humor

Why did the SQL query cross the road?

To join the chickens on the other side—with a LEFT JOIN, of course.

Why don't SQL databases ever get invited to parties?

Because they can't handle too many connections.

A DBA walks into a bar, a table, and a column.

It was a syntax error.

Why did the developer break up with the database?

Because every time they tried to commit, it would roll back emotionally.

What's an SQL query's favorite type of relationship?

One-to-many—because it's all about options.

Why did the SELECT statement go to therapy?

Too many INNER JOINs from its past.

Why did the database administrator get promoted?

Because she knew how to control access, maintain relationships, and always kept things normalized.

What did the SQL query say after breaking up with the table?

DELETE FROM relationships WHERE feelings = 'mutual';

Knock knock.

Who's there?

SELECT.

SELECT who?

SELECT * FROM people WHERE name = 'You';

Why did the query go broke?

It didn't use WHERE, so it spent everything.

How do SQL programmers fix broken relationships?

They use foreign keys and set ON DELETE CASCADE.

Final thought:

Love is like a LEFT JOIN... sometimes you're just waiting on the right match to appear.

14. Final Thoughts

Introduction

You've come a long way. From defining tables and executing SELECT statements to writing complex joins and managing transactions, you now have a comprehensive understanding of SQL and its ecosystem. This chapter ties everything together and equips you with a strategic mindset for what comes next. Whether your goal is to become a data engineer, an analyst, or simply a fluent problem-solver in the age of information, SQL is a tool you'll carry with you throughout your journey.

What You've Learned

Let's quickly reflect on your progress:

- **Chapter 1:** You learned that SQL isn't just a query language—it's a paradigm for organizing, retrieving, and managing structured data.
- **Chapter 2:** You explored SQL's five functional categories and saw how they work in concert: DDL, DML, DCL, TCL, and DQL.
- **Chapter 3:** You installed and connected to MySQL, the world's most popular open-source RDBMS.
- **Chapters 4–9:** You dove into each SQL category, learning syntax, workflows, and real-world use cases.
- **Chapter 10:** You discovered SQL dialects and how MySQL, PostgreSQL, SQL Server, and others interpret syntax slightly differently.
- **Chapter 11:** You expanded into advanced SQL topics like views, window functions, and common table expressions.
- **Chapter 12:** You peeked into NoSQL territory—learning that not all data fits neatly into relational tables.
- **Chapter 13:** You applied what you've learned through practical projects and real-world case studies.

The Mindset of a SQL Professional

Now that you've mastered the syntax and workflows, it's time to cultivate the habits of a database professional:

- **Think relationally.** Consider how data elements connect. Design tables to model relationships, not just rows.
- **Plan for scale.** Efficient schemas and well-thought indexing strategies pay off when your tables grow.
- **Expect failure.** Use transactions and constraints to guard against mistakes and ensure data integrity.
- **Stay curious.** Even seasoned DBAs Google syntax from time to time. Learning never stops.
- **Read execution plans.** SQL is declarative, but performance is technical. Know how to profile and tune.

Where to Go from Here

Here are ways to take your skills to the next level:

- **Learn by doing.** Build side projects. Reverse-engineer datasets. Write SQL every day.
- **Explore data analytics.** Tools like Tableau, Power BI, and Python's pandas integrate seamlessly with SQL.
- **Dig into PostgreSQL or SQL Server.** Get comfortable with different dialects and what makes each special.
- **Master indexes and performance tuning.** The difference between good and great SQL lies in efficiency.
- **Contribute to open datasets.** Sites like Kaggle, DataHub, and government portals offer great playgrounds.

Common Pitfalls to Avoid

- **Overusing SELECT** *. Always select only the fields you need—it saves bandwidth and keeps code readable.

- **Neglecting NULL logic.** Learn to anticipate NULL values in JOINs and WHERE clauses.
- **Forgetting transactions.** Use BEGIN, COMMIT, and ROLLBACK when manipulating data in bulk.
- **Hardcoding values.** Parameterize queries whenever possible, especially in apps.
- **Ignoring security.** Always lock down permissions with DCL and avoid SQL injection vulnerabilities.

Conclusion

SQL is more than a skill—it's a lens through which you can explore the hidden structure of everything digital. From websites to financial systems, medical records to shopping carts, SQL is behind it all. As data continues to shape the world around us, your fluency in this language becomes a kind of superpower. Use it wisely. Use it creatively. And most importantly, use it to bring clarity to complexity.

You've just finished Structured Query Language: SQL Concepts and Comic Relief. If this message spoke to you, share it with someone who needs to learn this subject matter.

Please take a moment to leave a review where you got this audiobook — it helps others discover the book and spreads the message further.

Thank you for listening and remember: your story isn't finished yet. Step forward with courage, live without apology, and know that you can manage data with SQL.

End-of-Book Humor

"I had a problem, so I used SQL. Now I have 1 table... and 2 problems."

Don't worry—by now, you know how to fix them both.

---

1. Queries are used to retrieve specific data, modify existing data (e.g., insert new records, update values, delete records), or even define and manage the database structure itself (e.g., create tables, indexes).↩

2. Data integrity refers to the accuracy, consistency, and reliability of data throughout its lifecycle. It ensures that data remains valid, complete, and unaltered, whether in storage, during processing, or in transit. Essentially, it's about maintaining the trustworthiness of data.↩
3. PHP is a widely used, open-source, server-side scripting language primarily designed for web development. It allows developers to create dynamic web pages by embedding code within Hyper Text Markup Language (HTML). PHP is known for its ability to handle server-side logic, interact with databases, and generate dynamic content that changes based on user input or other factors.↩
4. phpMyAdmin is a free and open-source web application written in PHP, designed to manage MySQL and MariaDB databases. It provides a user-friendly interface for performing various database operations, such as creating databases and tables, managing users and privileges, and executing SQL queries. It's a popular tool, especially in web hosting environments, as it simplifies database management compared to using the command-line interface.↩
5. While often expanded as the "Practical Extraction and Report Language", it's a retronym and not a true acronym as its creator, Larry Wall, came up with the name first. Perl is a high-level, general-purpose, interpreted, multi-paradigm, dynamic programming language. It was initially designed by Larry Wall in 1987, primarily for text manipulation and reporting tasks. Perl offers flexibility in programming styles, allowing for procedural, object-oriented, and functional approaches. Perl and PHP are both server-side scripting languages that have historically been used for web development.↩

www.ingramcontent.com/pod-product-compliance
Lightning Source LLC
LaVergne TN
LVHW022057200926
848481LV00003B/958